AYRTON SENNA

By the same author:

JAMES HUNT
Portrait of a champion

GERHARD BERGER
The human face of Formula 1

AYRTON SENNA
The hard edge of genius

TORVILL AND DEAN
The full story

TWO WHEEL SHOWDOWN!
The full drama of the races which decided
the World 500cc Motor Cycle Championship
from 1949

GRAND PRIX SHOWDOWN!
The full drama of the races which decided
the World Championship 1950–92

HONDA
Conquerors of the track

HONDA
The conquest of Formula 1

NIGEL MANSELL
The making of a champion

ALAIN PROST

A MAN CALLED MIKE

Patrick Stephens Limited, an imprint of Haynes Publishing, has published authoritative, quality books for enthusiasts for more than 25 years. During that time the company has established a reputation as one of the world's leading publishers of books on aviation, maritime, military, model-making, motor cycling, motoring, motor racing, railway and railway modelling subjects. Readers or authors with suggestions for books they would like to see published are invited to write to: The Editorial Director, Patrick Stephens Limited, Sparkford, Nr. Yeovil, Somerset BA22 7JJ.

AYRTON SENNA

INCORPORATING 'THE SECOND COMING'

Christopher Hilton

PSL

Patrick Stephens Limited

First published in April 1994
Reprinted in May 1994
incorporating *The Second Coming*
Reprinted in June 1994

British Library cataloguing-in-publication data:
A catalogue record for this book is
available from the British Library.

ISBN: 1 85260 483 2

Library of Congress catalog card no: 93 81195

Patrick Stephens Limited is an imprint of Haynes Publishing,
Sparkford, Nr. Yeovil, Somerset BA22 7JJ.

Typeset by G&M, Raunds, Northamptonshire.
Printed in Great Britain by Butler & Tanner Ltd, London and Frome.

Contents

Introduction

THIS IS THE book Ayrton Senna never read, and I regret that as I mourn him. It was published just before his shocking death in the San Marino Grand Prix at Imola on 1 May 1994.

The book is a celebration of an immense talent. It is also, I hope, a complete record of the last three years of his racing life up to his joining the Rothmans Williams team. I ask you, the reader, to approach it in that knowledge. The words written before his death have been left alone.

He liked my first biography, *Ayrton Senna: The Hard Edge of Genius*, and I believe he would have wished that this latest book be available to those who followed his career with such dedication.

This revised edition completes the story, examining the crash and its global repercussions. Written with affection, and including Senna's own insights, and the comments of those who worked with him and drove against him, it is, I hope, a fitting tribute.

The book is an exploration of Senna leaving Marlboro McLaren and joining Rothmans Williams Renault; an exploration of a complete contradiction, how he wielded his maturity to lead Championships and win races in a car barely capable of that — authentic greatness.

I've recreated the races in detail, particularly the 1993 European

Grand Prix at Donington, because the full depth of his creativity lay within them. Wherever possible I've used the words he spoke at the time to give an insight into his thinking and demonstrate how each practice, each qualifying, each Grand Prix was a delicate, sometimes maddening search among many equilibriums — engine, chassis, aerodynamics, tyres, circuit, weather, grid position, race position, mental state, physical state, the endless variables always in play in the search — and how he mastered them or they mastered him. Woven into this are other people's insights, reflections and refractions.

But — probably alone in a sport reported by men for men — this book also offers a poignant insight into the impact Senna made on women of all ages, cultures and nationalities. Following publication of *The Hard Edge of Genius* I received a number of letters from women who saw in him strange mystical as well as sexual powers. Here, writing before his death of course, they speak for themselves — from the heart.

In no particular order I thank the following for their time, their thoughts or their help: Ron Dennis, Jo Ramirez and Peter Stayner of McLaren International; Frank Williams, Damon Hill, Ann Bradshaw and Richard West of Williams Grand Prix Engineering Limited; Martin Brundle; Mark Blundell; Nick Harris, Sue Coggs and Shirley Robinson of Rothmans (UK) Limited; Katie Sore and Proaction; Vicky Canas of *El Pais*; Gerald Sezille of Tag Heuer and Rolendo Orgentero of Olivetti; Nigel Roebuck and Tony Dodgins of *Autosport*; Derick Allsop of *The Independent*; Malcolm Folley of *The Mail On Sunday*. In the chapter titled *Cries From The Heart*, I'm grateful to the following for permission to reproduce their feelings about Senna: Laura Giglio, Lyn Patey, Carolynne Kristina, Renee Sharp, Paulina Markovic and Evelyn Ong.

I'm grateful to Betise Assumpdao who handled being a conduit to him with good humour and finesse.

The first quotation in *Cries From The Heart* is taken from *Grand Prix People* by Gerald Donaldson (published by MRP).

The bulk of the photographs are by LAT, and thanks to Cathy Ager for the usual superb service.

CHAPTER ONE

The Final Corner

IMMEDIATELY AFTER THE impact, the world we had known grew darker, moment by moment. The golden helmet did not move within the cockpit, and movement — any movement — is what you look for first because it means life. Even when careful hands laid him on the ground beside the savaged wreck of his car there was still no movement. An ambulance waited to take him to the track's medical centre, the normal route to examination, recuperation, rehabilitation. The careful hands did not put him in the ambulance. They carried him to the helicopter which had landed on the track and, like the ambulance, waited. The helicopter would take him direct to the Maggiore Hospital, Bologna. I think I knew then.

The darkness deepened. Bulletins spoke of his condition as critical, spoke of a coma, of major brain damage, that he was clinically dead and then, at 6.40pm local time, that he had died.

Ayrton Senna was 34.

Across the years he had changed the world we had known and now, in his leaving, he changed it again. He left a void which some tried to fill by tears or fighting back tears, some by silence, some by fevered speculation about the events which ended at a corner called Tamburello on lap seven of the San Marino Grand Prix, Imola, 1 May 1994; some by rewinding the whole race meeting, searching for

The moody charisma of the man. It is how he will be remembered (ICN UK Bureau).

clues, raking over the nuances of every word he'd said; some by simply going away to accept the finality in their solitude.

I wonder if they found the acceptance. I wonder if some of them ever will.

The instants, hours and days which followed seemed to tumble over each other in a bewildering cascade, drawn into dimension after dimension. There would be open grief at the gates of the Williams Grand Prix Engineering factory in Didcot, where strangers came to lay flowers. In his native Brazil the grief was communal. Men, women and children did not fight back tears as the country passed towards three days of official mourning. But to appreciate the scale of Senna you must speak of global grief.

The dimensions embraced an autopsy, the Chief Executive of the San Marino circuit being placed under supervisory arrest, the impounding of the Williams car, and the news that its 'black box' had been found, which might help ease the fevered speculation. But the scale of Senna pitched the accident higher and higher. There was a rising clamour about safety, not just of Tamburello but the whole of Imola; not just about the Williams but all Formula 1 cars, about helmets and protection for the neck. There were the questions which always stab-stab-stab after a fatality, but now more and more urgent under the scale of Senna. *Should there be motorsport at all? Will it survive? Should it survive?* But none of this masked the immediate question, the one centred on the few seconds of lap seven of the San Marino Grand Prix.

Why?

Ayrton Senna left the Marlboro McLaren team to join Rothmans Williams Renault for 1994; he'd partner Damon Hill. The Williams car seemed invincible and it took Nigel Mansell to the 1992 World Championship, Alain Prost to the 1993 World Championship. Senna had shaped his teenage years and adult life to winning, and — as it seemed — the Williams car would remain invincible. He went there. It was not quite as callous and calculating as that; something we'll come to.

In Brazil, the opening race of 1994, Senna was decisively outpowered by the young German Michael Schumacher in his Benetton Ford, and spun out. Moments after the start of the next race, the Pacific Grand Prix at a new circuit, Aida, Japan, he was nudged from behind, nudged off. Schumacher won.

Huge pressure faced Senna as he approached San Marino. His very presence at Williams had excited great anticipation inside and outside the team, and it remained unfulfilled. He was being outdriven by a younger man for the first time in his life and, moreover, a man nearly a decade younger. Even if Senna won San Marino from Schumacher — something which might be very, very difficult — Schumacher still led the Championship 26 points to 10. If Senna didn't win, the Championship, which only weeks before had offered itself as virtually a formality, became a mountain climb riven with hazardous colls, overhangs and icy gullies.

Moreover, Formula 1's rules had changed to eliminate the sophisticated driver aids like anti-lock brakes and traction control. In theory, that returned the skills of driving to the driver. In practice it appeared to make the cars more awkward to control. Senna spoke of these changes as ill-advised. 'It is going to be a season with a lot of accidents. I will even risk saying that if something really serious doesn't happen we will be lucky.'

In the aftermath those words would be endlessly recycled into a haunting, harrowing premonition. They stab-stab-stabbed from television screens, loomed from teletext services, whispered down Press wire services, echoed from radio stations, shrieked from newspaper headlines. But not on Thursday, 28 April when the drivers began to arrive at Imola, a gentle, verdant town of fading splendours, and contemplated the first day of qualifying, the Friday: another race in another place. Maybe some wondered about the surface of the track, which traditionally was bumpy — an alarming consideration for the margins of a Formula 1 car — but it had been resurfaced at strategic places.

Sixteen minutes into that qualifying session, the Brazilian Rubens Barrichello lost control of his Sasol Jordan at the Variante Bassa, a snap of a right-hander before the pit lane entrance. The car rode the kerbing, wisps of smoke rose from it as Barrichello jabbed the brakes, but the angle of the kerbing launched it. The car became a missile skimming the top of the tyre barrier before it hammered the steel protective fencing behind. Under the impact the car recoiled from that and somersaulted. The safety services reacted quickly and Barrichello was taken the normal route, to the track medical centre for examination and then Maggiore Hospital. He had no more than a broken nose and a broken rib.

'I remember exactly the moment before I touched the barrier,' Barrichello would say, 'waiting for the crash and then everything went into darkness. The next thing I knew I was in the medical centre with Senna there. Senna was the first person to visit me at the hospital.' When the session resumed, Senna's team-mate Damon Hill went out and spun. How awkward were these cars to control? A few moments later Martin Brundle, in a Marlboro McLaren Peugeot, spun at the spoon-shaped Rivazza corner. How awkward were these cars . . ?

Senna took provisional pole, one minute 21.648 seconds against Schumacher's one minute 22.015. Senna described the session as 'a bit chaotic' after Barrichello's accident, 'but I think the result is excellent, given the circumstances. I don't feel that I ever drove the car properly. I was out there when he had the accident and after that I wasn't driving well, not consistent, not able to do it properly. It was just myself not being able to concentrate.'

Mark Fogarty of *Carweek* waited patiently for Senna to emerge from the motorhome to interview him about his growing business empire. 'It must have been six o'clock-ish,' Fogarty says. 'He'd been in a lengthy debrief. We spoke for about 15 or 20 minutes in a corner of the hospitality area. He seemed detached, not at all his usual focused self. In any interview he often hesitated for a long time before answering a question while he worked out exactly what he wanted to say. Now he hesitated much longer than normal. He looked extremely tired, eyes red and glassy, he looked drawn. He was obviously not happy with the car. He said "we have a big engineering problem with it. When my race engineer comes back I'll have to go and talk to him". That's what happened. Ayrton excused himself and said we'd continue the interview after Saturday qualifying.'

Eighteen minutes into the Saturday session Roland Ratzenberger in a Simtek Ford — a new Formula 1 team — reached towards 200mph at the Villeneuve corner just before the spoon-shaped Tosa, perhaps the fastest point on the whole circuit. It seemed that a front wing came off. The 31-year-old Austrian struck the left-hand wall with a frantic ferocity and the car came to rest some 200 yards further on. The helmet did not move within the cockpit. He was given emergency treatment at the trackside before they took him to the medical centre and then by helicopter to the Maggiore. He died soon after.

It was the first death at a Grand Prix meeting for 12 years, specifically, since Canada, on 13 June 1982. Of all the drivers at Imola on Saturday, 30 April 1994, only two — Andrea de Cesaris (Sasol Jordan) and Michele Alboreto (Minardi) — had been present that desperate, dreadful, destructive day in Canada. The era without a death stretched across as broad a span as that. The effect of Ratzenberger's death was therefore commensurately profound. None of the other drivers, including Senna, had had to cope with it before.

Neither the McLaren nor Benetton teams resumed when the session began again, but Gerhard Berger in the Ferrari did. 'I was sitting in my car watching the pictures of the accident on the portable television screen. I could see how bad it was. I knew how critical the situation looked. For the first time I found myself shaking after an accident. In our job you have to be prepared to see situations like this, but because the driver was Austrian and a personal friend, it was worse.

'You shouldn't differentiate between drivers like that, but this does affect you in a different way. I felt sick. I got out of the car and went to the motorhome where I was still shaking. You ask yourself whether you want to drive or not. The question is about racing. It is not related to this afternoon and it would not make any difference to Roland. But yesterday, when I saw Rubens Barrichello's accident, it made me realise how close we are to life and death. So you ask these questions. Then you say "yes, I am going to race on Sunday". So you go out and try to concentrate on the job. It was difficult, it was very hard.' Consider it: in 1989, driving a Ferrari, Berger went off at Tamburello — something on the car broke and after it had beaten itself into pieces against the concrete wall, a fireball from hell consumed the remnants. That Berger survived was due to the speed of response, the courage and expertise of the rescue services as well as the inherent strength of the car.

The death of Ratzenberger affected Senna and Hill visibly.

'Late Saturday,' Fogarty says, 'I literally bumped into Ayrton. I didn't have to say anything, I just looked at him. "I'm not talking to anyone," he said. "Give me a call later in the week and we'll do it over the telephone." He looked very distracted.'

Late that night Senna telephoned his girlfriend, Adriene Galisteu, a 21-year-old model holidaying at his home in southern Portugal. Adriene's mother subsequently described Senna's conversation: 'I am not in a very good state of mind. These two accidents have left me deeply depressed. If there was any way I could avoid running in the race I would, but I have to go on'. There seems little doubt that Senna genuinely loved Adriene, although — except at heightened moments at race tracks — he exercised as much control over his emotions as he did over a car.

Only a few days before Imola, Senna said: 'Even when you are beside a woman that you love, you might think she could make you unhappy in the future. The relationship between a man and a woman is the oldest thing that exists in humanity, and there are still no formulae to guarantee love, peace, and the success of a relationship. For this reason a relationship must be valued day by day. It is not only the dream that most of us have but the reality that we must evaluate'. Maybe Senna remembered his first marriage which ended in divorce a decade and more before when, incidentally, Michael Schumacher was aged 12: the broad span of time again.

And so we come to Sunday, 1 May. Prost was present as a television commentator on a French channel, and during the morning

13

warm-up session Senna said over the on-board radio 'a special hello to my dear friend Alain — we'll miss you, now you've retired from driving!' They'd battled and snarled and crashed in the past. They'd convulsed Grand Prix racing by their mutual loathing, they'd patched it up and now, on a spring morning at the gentle town, the healing was complete.

Before the start of the Grand Prix Senna shook hands with Prost who'd say 'we were rivals and even more than that. We were not friends, but maybe we can be friends in the future'. Subsequently Prost added: 'I noticed Ayrton had a strange, almost bizarre look about him'.

The start of the San Marino Grand Prix went wrong in the way any start can go wrong. You have twin columns of cars placed close together revving mighty engines, and at the instant of unleashing — the green light — you have a compression of reaction, acceleration, jostling and chancing which is rodeo. If anything goes wrong the margins are milli-seconds, if that. Perhaps instantaneous combustion is a better way of putting it.

J. J. Lehto's Benetton, on the third row of the grid, stalled. The column of cars behind Lehto weaved and flicked past until a young Portuguese, Pedro Lamy (Lotus) rode his chance in the rodeo and sliced across from the other column, was unsighted by a car ahead and struck the Benetton a terrible blow, punting it. 'I had no chance to avoid him,' Lamy said. 'I saw a space to the left and went for it.' The impact wrenched wheels from the Lotus and hurled them over the debris fence into the crowd. A wheel just missed a man running away but struck a policeman and three spectators. One was hurt so severely he went into a coma. Lehto and Lamy were unhurt.

The race had gone by then, Senna (pole) leading from Schumacher, although Schumacher thought Senna's Williams looked 'nervous'.

What followed is hard to understand. Wreckage and debris lay who knows where, and you'd expect the race to be stopped, and restarted later when the track had been carefully and calmly cleared. That's the way it used to be. But since 1992, if there is an accident, a saloon safety vehicle is sent out to lead the cars slowly round in a crocodile until any obstruction on the track has been dealt with.

The saloon emerged and the crocodile followed, cars darting from side to side to keep the tyres warm. The saloon had bright, rotating

The start of the fatal race, Imola, 1 May 1994 (ICN UK Bureau).

After a start line crash, they followed the safety car. When it released them Senna's own crash was only moments away (ICN UK Bureau).

The savage aftermath (Allsport).

lights on its roof, and the moment these were extinguished it meant *the track is now clear and we will complete another lap, I'll pull off and you race again with a rolling start.* The race was resumed on lap six. As the saloon peeled off, Senna and Schumacher got onto the power fast, so fast they drew instantly away from Berger, third in the crocodile.

Schumacher did as a racer would, moved on Senna, tried to crowd him, looked for a position to overtake. Whether the overt and inverted pressures on Senna were material in what followed will never now be known. I remember thinking, as Schumacher began the crowding, that Senna would resist it and that might take Senna to the limit. There was nowhere else for Senna to go. He could have surrendered to a superior force — Schumacher — but he'd have violated all that his life meant if he'd done that. Should the moment come when it was utterly impossible to resist, he might move aside, but that moment would be far from the lap six they were on. The San Marino Grand Prix was still a new-born child, with innumerable permutations to play themselves out: another race, another place, 52 laps to run, a lifetime of possibilities.

In tandem Senna and Schumacher crossed the line to complete lap six, and travelled into lap seven, travelled the short lunge to Tamburello, this foot-down surge of an uncoiling left-hander which came at you like a slap in the face, this on-the-rim-of-the-universe corner which made so many drivers talk to themselves as they approached it, perhaps to talk themselves into approaching it.

Senna did not soothe the Williams into the left-hander to make this an ordinary corner, one he had been passing through since 1985. He did not angle the Williams and caress it to precisely the angle he wanted, nicely near the rim of the universe but a guarded, safe distance away from that. He did not appear even to twist it or wrestle it in an instinctive attempt to alter direction. He went straight on. The Williams crossed the run-off area shedding speed but not enough speed.

Ayrton Senna must have seen the concrete wall poised to swallow him then, mercifully, there would be nothing except darkness. From leaving the track to reaching the wall took less than a second and then, if what he always believed was true, he would meet the God he felt he had known for so long. Of the physical world after the impact — the car flung from the wall, flung back to the track — he would have known nothing.

The greatest driver in the world, and perhaps the greatest driver of all time, had careful, sensitive hands which had soothed many cars in many situations. Within a moment or two careful, sensitive hands would tend his own body and pass it to other careful, sensitive hands until it reached the Morumbi Cemetery in Sao Paulo five days later.

The Williams looked like a butchered carcass — but the cockpit survived. In the most poignant sense that didn't matter, because the golden helmet leaning so slackly against the headrest did not move.

After the impact the instants tumbled into hours which tumbled into days, so I propose to set it down in chronological order and with, I trust, full respect. There are many medical details of Senna's accident which are hellish. You will not be reading them here.

Adriene Galisteu watched the race on television in Portugal. A friend with a jet offered to fly her to Italy but when the plane was airborne the control tower radioed the news that Senna was dead. The plane returned and she prepared to fly direct to Sao Paulo.

Jackie Stewart, the former World Champion who launched the campaign for safety in Formula 1 in the 1960s, was at Silverstone where his son Paul's team competed in a Formula 3 race. Jim Dunn of *The Scotsman* had arranged to interview Stewart so he could write a story about Formula 1 safety based around Ratzenberger's crash and now that of Senna, although at this moment neither Dunn nor Stewart were aware of the full horror. By an impossible irony, Stewart explained how he had repeatedly urged Senna to take the lead in driver and circuit safety as the man officials would have to listen to. Stewart and Dunn sat in a small room at the rear of the Press area. Someone came in and said 'there's news about Senna. I'm sorry. It's not good'.

For a long moment Stewart gazed at his hands. 'We've had this long period of relative safety and I think that people have maybe grown dangerously complacent about the risks. Something will have to be done to reduce the speed of the cars. The passive safety, witnessed by the speed with which help was rushed to Senna, is excellent too, but we can never be complacent. I think now the authorities will have to look at the design of modern high-speed tracks such as Imola. No matter how good the safety of the cars and the equipment, the human body just cannot stand the G-forces generated in these high-speed crashes. The body can survive up to 66 times the force of gravity, but after that . . .'

There was a San Marino Grand Prix on 1 May 1994 after the wreckage of Senna's accident had been cleared. Towards the end of it Alboreto's Minardi lost a wheel exiting the pit lane after a tyre stop, and the wheel struck four mechanics. Mercifully only one received real injury, a broken knee. Michael Schumacher won the 'race'. They sprayed no champagne on the winners' balcony. Later, Schumacher would say that 'Ayrton took two or three bumps. I was behind and, the lap before, I saw he was a little unstable and skittish in that corner. The next time he went sideways and then he lost it'.

A crowd estimated at 30,000 gathered at the Maggiore Hospital, so many that his body could not be removed for an autopsy. When the race was over, spectators went to the scene of the accident to search for souvenirs. In Sao Paulo police protected the office block where Senna ran his business in case distraught members of his fan club — there watching the race — tried to remove souvenirs.

Monday, 2 May
Members of the Williams team flew back to England on Sunday night, landing shortly after midnight. Ann Bradshaw, the team's highly experienced Press Relations Officer, faced a television camera 'because you have to. You can't run away from what happened'. She spoke a few sombre words but her face betrayed her feelings. She looked as if she had come from another planet.

That morning the British headlines brushed aside news of the first full South African election, regarded as a turning point in 20th century democracy. That was equally true in Italy where, with very little restraint, newspapers apportioned blame, passing judgement on the circuit, the crash helmets, the Williams team.

That morning, too, mourners made their way to the Williams factory to position bouquets on the gates. The team's Commercial Director, Richard West, said: 'A little boy arrived here first thing with some flowers. He'd probably only ever seen Ayrton on TV, but Ayrton meant everything to him. When sport loses someone like Ayrton, millions of people around the world feel it even though they have never met him'.

Frank Williams, who'd remained in Italy, arrived in the early after-noon, his eyes reddened, and was driven into the factory without stopping. He'd need time to choose his words. When he was ready he said: 'Williams Grand Prix Engineering is a family, and although Ayrton had only joined us this season, he and I enjoyed a longstanding relationship, and I am proud that the first Formula 1 car he ever drove was indeed a Williams. He gave us his total commitment, and we gave him ours. He loved his motor racing and shared this passion with every one of our employees at Didcot. We are a Grand Prix team, committed to the sport, and will continue our work, which I am sure is exactly what Ayrton would have wanted. He became a key member of our team in a very short time, and I hope that what we achieve in the future will be an honour to his memory.

'His loss is impossible to quantify. Everyone who has ever met him in whatever capacity feels they have lost someone very special. All of us in the Rothmans Williams Renault team will remember him with respect, admiration and affection. Our sincere condolences go to his family and many friends around the world.

'We are at this moment studying data available to us to ascertain the cause of the accident. The FIA, motorsport's governing body, as a matter of policy investigates all accidents and they too will be examining all the relevant information'.

The FIA announced that they had arranged a meeting in Paris for Wednesday. They said that 'the FIA is gathering reports from its technical, medical, safety and supervisory staff, as well as from the relevant team and circuit personnel. As soon as these reports are received, they will be studied as a matter of urgency'.

Jean Todt, Manager of Ferrari, said in Italy that work would begin immediately on improved crash helmets, not just to protect the driver's head but his neck as well. 'We will give twice what it costs, it is as important as that. At the moment we know that the driver's body is protected by a strong chassis, and there has been a great improvement in circuit safety. It is obvious that the weak point is the driver's head. Helmets are heavy and subject to enormous deceleration, and nothing has been done to protect the back of the neck. For me, that is a major concern.'

Before the San Marino Grand Prix, Prost had spoken of how in Formula 1 'everything is done for business, for money, and nothing for the sport'. Max Mosley, President of the FIA, countered that. 'The truth of the matter is that, generally speaking, drivers are interested

The day after. Stunned supporters pay their homage and last respects at the gates of the Williams factory (Times Newspapers Ltd).

in having the fastest car. They are not really interested in safety. That is our responsibility, and something to which we give constant thought and attention.'

In Italy, magistrates ordered the autopsies on Senna and Ratzenberger to be carried out, impounded the cars, and sealed the circuit. They confiscated all film of the race. There was talk of possible criminal proceedings, embracing the track manager, Williams officials, and Simtek.

Grief hung over Brazil. The country's President, Itamar Franco, declared three days of national mourning and cancelled his official engagements. The Foreign Minister, Celso Amorim, tried to hasten the release of Senna's body and offered his plane to bring it home, but the Bologna magistrates insisted on the autopsy on Tuesday morning. One of Senna's former girlfriends, Marcella Praddo, claimed her baby daughter was Senna's love child. The taking up of positions for Senna's millions had begun.

Tuesday, 3 May
Headlines shrieked again, like SENNA: HIS FATAL ERROR. Williams Technical Director Patrick Head had been quoted by Italian

and Brazilian newspapers as saying 'Ayrton Senna made a mistake. We have checked the telemetry. He slightly lifted his foot just at the dip in the place where the tarmac changes. That caused a loss of downforce to the rear wing which meant the car went straight on'.

Quietly, in the background, Damon Hill paid his tribute. 'For all his concerns about safety, Ayrton never played safe in the cockpit. He performed at a hundred per cent all the time and for that he commanded admiration from every driver. I will never forget my short period working with him, and consider myself immensely privileged to have been a team-mate. The loss of Roland and Ayrton has affected everyone deeply.'

Quietly, in the background, Senna's body was flown to Paris so that it could be transferred to an overnight flight to Sao Paulo and the long, last journey to the place he loved most of all.

Wednesday, 4 May
A guard of honour waited as the Varig plane landed at dawn from leaden skies. Six airforce cadets loaded the coffin on to a large hearse — in fact a fire engine — and it began its dignified procession to the laying in state at the Sao Paulo legislative assembly. Six motorcycle riders formed a phalanx around it, others formed an arrowhead before it. As the cortege reached the city, uniformed cavalry replaced the bike riders, and now it moved so slowly that thousands upon thousands ran parallel to it as if they wanted to accompany it. Perhaps a million people saw the cortege pass. At the legislative assembly an immense crowd waited, many waving flags in mute salute. Here, 16 uniformed men carried the coffin slowly along a red carpet and between massive white pillars into the building. The coffin was draped in the blue, green and gold of Brazil. Some quarter of a million people were expected to file past the coffin before the funeral on Thursday.

At Didcot, Williams issued a statement. 'Following reports in the Press that the Rothmans Williams Renault team blames Ayrton Senna for Sunday's accident, Technical Director Patrick Head has commented: "We are still studying the data, still gathering the information, and at this stage we have reached no conclusions. All the relevant information is not available at present. I believe that any initial conversations I had at the circuit have been taken out of context, and would point out that I have not spoken to any journalists on the subject since leaving the circuit. At no time did I ever say Ayrton Senna was to blame".'

In Paris the FIA met, and then Mosley faced the Press. *Shouldn't the remainder of the season be called off?* 'It would be I think overreacting in the absence of some evidence. Everyone has been deeply affected by what happened over the weekend at Imola. We are confronted with problems in motorsport, but we have to keep our calm and sang-froid. We need to examine the cars to be able to come to precise conclusions as to the causes of the accidents. This will only be available in about a month from now. What I can tell you now is that each of the three accidents of the weekend — Barrichello, Ratzenberger and Senna — are unconnected.

'Alain Prost has suggested, among other people, that the Federation has no contact with the drivers and is in some way distant from the drivers. This is completely untrue. This suggestion has only been made by people seeking to make trouble. We have worked constantly on means to improve safety for the last three years and next year. One of the areas under examination is airbags for front impact.

'The immediate safety measures we can make for the Monaco Grand Prix (two weeks after Imola) will concern the pit lanes. They are the following: 1) The entrance and exit to the pit lane will be shaped to decelerate the cars, thus reducing the number of pit stops because of the time loss. 2) It will be prohibited for anyone to stand in the pit lane unless they are about to work on a car or have just finished. 3) We will ensure that the number of cars that come in on each lap is very limited. The unscheduled stops will not be for changing tyres or refuelling.'

Thursday, 5 May
They laid him to rest with great dignity. Berger and Prost and Stewart and Emerson Fittipaldi and Hill helped bear the coffin, their faces drawn, sombre, perhaps still uncomprehending. Others of his life were here also, Frank Williams, Ron Dennis of Marlboro McLaren. Petals were strewn over the coffin before its lowering. Field guns fired a salute and far, far overhead, jets carved a huge 'S' in the sky. Ayrton Senna da Silva was buried in the Morumbi Cemetery in the centre of a large, circular plot.

It is precisely the shape of a wheel.

The Final Words

Ayrton Senna was an extraordinary racing driver. His skills, craft, subtlety and courage were of such magnitude that he dwarfed his generation of drivers. With McLaren he won three World Championships, and in doing so gave pleasure not only to all of us in the team but to millions of people. But to me he was more than all of this, more than a World Champion, more than a successful businessman. To me he was a friend.

Friendships are born in so many ways, and mean different things to different people. Ayrton and I fought a lot, argued even more and at times even ignored each other. This is because we were both consumed by the same will to win, and to do so fairly. Out of our shared passion grew mutual respect. Yet we still tried to beat one another. In the end we realised we were as stubborn and committed as each other. That is when our friendship began. Slowly at first, it became even stronger.

This friendship, born in the heat of battle to succeed, meant a lot to me. Normally I am not an emotional man. Nor was Ayrton. But we both found depths of emotion when we went Grand Prix racing together. I shall miss him greatly.

— Ron Dennis, McLaren International

I am in a total state of shock — as I am sure everyone in motor racing is — at this horrific loss of life. I was stunned after the Austrian driver, Roland Ratzenberger, was killed and for Ayrton to lose his life the very next day makes this particular weekend a very black weekend in motor racing history.

Ayrton and I shared some of the most exciting races ever staged, and it is impossible to put into words what a sad loss to motor racing this is, because when a truly great driver and a great champion loses his life, there is a very big void left behind.

I send my sincere condolences to the family and friends of both Ayrton Senna and

Roland Ratzenberger and I know, having driven for the Williams team for six years, how they must be feeling. My thoughts, sympathy and understanding are with them, too. I can only add that there is not a driver in the world who will not be shocked and deeply affected by this terrible news. — Nigel Mansell

I always had a good relationship with him in our brief encounters. Senna was very good to us. He was supportive of Michael (Andretti). In fact, his was one of the first congratulatory messages Michael got after Michael won in Australia (first IndyCar race of 1994 in March). Quite honestly, I don't know what else to say. It comes as a tremendous shock to all of us. It's a devastating loss. — Mario Andretti

I knew him first-hand and 99 per cent of the things you read about Senna weren't true. He was a very good person, supportive of me and all the problems I had. He was one of the guys who really stuck up for me. — Michael Andretti

The water's up today and I'd love to be out on my surfboard. I want to be doing something. As I'm looking outside, Ayrton's death has made me realise that you've got to live each day and enjoy it. I thought the guy was immortal. I really did. He was going to be an icon and he was going to end his days on the beach, windsurfing. Like me he was a Pisces and he understood the water thing. Wordsworth said, 'Good times, bad times, these are the only times'. What happened to Ayrton makes you realise how we all waste too much time worrying about the future.
— Dennis Rushen, Senna's F2000 team manager

The death of Ayrton Senna at Imola on Sunday, May 1, has stunned the entire Renault organisation. Renault personnel, sharing a love for motor racing, are united in their grief at the loss of this great champion, who carried the Renault colours with style, expertise and the will to win which characterised this remarkable racing driver.
Louis Schweitzer, Renault Chairman, was present at the Grand Prix and after expressing his dismay, added: 'We must take action to eliminate all unnecessary risks. Formula 1 is a technological competition and has everything to gain from enhanced safety. We should work together to achieve this without delay.' — Renault Motor Sport

Jimmy Clark was basically a farmer who went motor racing. Stirling Moss enjoyed life to the full outside racing. I had my family and clay pigeon shooting outside the sport. Ayrton only had his racing and was 100 per cent dedicated and always had been. When I say 100 per cent I mean 99.9 per cent to just a few decimals away. — Jackie Stewart

The life of Ayrton Senna was an example of dedication and the love of the sport as few sportspeople have had at international level. The world lost the greatest athlete in the history of motor racing and I have lost a great friend. Grand Prix racing will never be the same without Ayrton. — Emerson Fittipaldi

• CHAPTER TWO •

Trading Places

A SALLOW SUN came sharp and sudden over the top lip of the concrete stand. A scurry of people eddied among the transporters which butted on to the pits, going nowhere in particular, milling, waiting. Ten thirty of a winter morning, and something's happening and nothing's happening.

Someone wearing a Rothmans anorak like a uniform announces urgently 'don't let anyone speak to *him*, no questions, absolutely no questions'. Wherever he goes these days there is one clear sense. Siege. *He* arrives, seemingly from nowhere, cloaked in a Rothmans anorak himself, *his* new uniform: a man of medium height, a thicket of dark, curling hair. He holds a certain balanced tension even in the act of walking. He'd respond to anything unexpected instantly, never losing the balance, and you've felt the same about Carl Lewis, Linford Christie, Muhammad Ali, Pele, Eusebio . . .

He has donned his molten, melting perma-smile and as he's chaperoned towards one of the transporters he calls out 'Hi, how are you?' I have to call back 'Sorry, can't answer any questions, not allowed!' The perma-smile opens into laughter. He sees what the siege has brought and why, and perhaps the irony of it; and still he holds the balance.

Estoril, January 1994. The sun is now refracting over the flinty hillocks which rise like a backdrop of vast, broken teeth.

He has already sampled the Williams Renault the day before. Today he'll give a demonstration run or two so that some 350 journalists and photographers can witness it. He won't work himself or the car hard. Tomorrow — the siege lifted, most of the 350 gone home — he'll take the first steps on the journey to knowing the car, its engine and the team. He'll say, quietly, that each move across the decade thus far — beginning in Formula 1 with Toleman, Toleman to Lotus, Lotus to McLaren — gave the career a kick, an acceleration. Here would be the next one.

Mid-morning and no car circled, the feeling of nothing and something lingering. An empty motor racing circuit is a curious contradiction. You wander the start-finish straight expecting one of those rockets to come round the spoon of a corner on to the straight, rising to an immense speed, and subconsciously you're listening for that, the shriek-gurgle of an engine announcing it. You'd forgotten how narrow this start-finish straight is, forgotten its pronounced slope towards Turn One, how sharply Turn One veers out of sight. You'd forgotten how pronounced the stagger of each row of the grid is, how much of an advantage pole position bestows. But the white symmet-

A new team and a new era. Senna shakes hands with 1994 team-mate Damon Hill.

rical bays are as empty as the circuit. They'll be filled within a few minutes — statically.

On that grid *he* poses with his new team-mate, Damon Hill, and his new car, the arc of photographers so numerous that a photographer takes a picture of the photographers and a magazine uses it, consciously charting the extent of the siege. Then he and Hill do go out and circle the track. They come past the pit lane wall in a flying formation in order that the photographers may have them in shot together.

Later he'll explain 'it is always a temptation to go faster and push harder to make better times, but given the conditions — very cold, a car new to me and we're getting over 320kph (198mph) on the straight — it takes a lot of careful self-control not to try and exploit the potential the car really has. By that, I mean you'd be exposing yourself to a potential accident, which is not the purpose at this stage'.

Is that part of growing up, that you don't have to prove you can get a thunderous time straight away, as you would have done when you started with Toleman in 1984?

'Yes, and I'm not just speaking about 10 years ago. Even six years ago I would have been trying harder at this stage, maybe taking the mental aspect a bit too far. Naturally I have been learning in these past six years and this is the biggest change I have had. Now I must use the experience.'

The choice of Estoril to launch Senna, Williams and the team's new sponsor, Rothmans, was entirely fortuitous, Estoril being a favoured haunt for Formula 1 testing and in theory a warm, dry place. This January day, however, the sun warmed by implication only.

Fortuitous? Here in 1984 Niki Lauda won the World Championship, an event of such magnitude that before the Portuguese Grand Prix several drivers said they'd get out of his way, wouldn't be seen to impede The Living Legend. But *he* — Senna — had said he wouldn't get out of the way, it would be up to The Living Legend to do it for himself.

Here in only the second race of 1985 *he* rode a storm and brought the Lotus home for his first victory and the team's first for three parched years, the sodden mechanics dancing in delight. He'd explain that everyone thought he exercised perfect control over the car but at one point he'd had all four wheels on the grass, his fate entirely in the lap of God.

Here in 1988 *he* came down this same pit lane straight wheel-to-wheel with Alain Prost and moved over on him, a frantically frightening instant or two, and in the Marlboro McLaren motorhome afterwards Prost said to Ayrton, '*I didn't realise you wanted the Championship that badly*'.

Here only a year further on, Nigel Mansell didn't see a black flag and — the McLaren pit trying to tell Senna *ignore Mansell, he's out of the race* — they crashed and a great reverberating rancour followed.

Here in 1991 Mansell's pit stop for tyres went desperately wrong, a wheel coming off as he accelerated down this pit lane, and he came to rest against the pit lane wall just over there. It virtually guaranteed Senna a third Championship.

Now, this chilled January day in 1994, he'll say 'I believe, even having done the 10 years of Formula 1 and won three World Championships, that the challenge to learn and improve yourself is the biggest motivating factor for me. As you go along, every year it becomes more and more difficult to motivate yourself to do a number of things which you don't normally enjoy' (the slog of normal winter testing, for example).

'Therefore these big changes in my career are like someone moving home. You have to find out everything, adjust everything, adjust yourself to it, get to know your new neighbours and make new friends. It is a way of motivating myself to keep up with the competitive level which Formula 1 requires from you.'

Do you think you can continue the good relationship you have with Damon throughout the season?

'Perfectly possible, although it is never easy because we are always competing, but I understand your question. We have those questions before we start any partnership with any of our colleagues, and perhaps I should say one thing. The only driver I have ever had problems with as a team-mate is Alain Prost. With the others, we raced hard and so occasionally we had our different opinions, but we were able to sort it out, sit down and discuss and have respect for each other. We also had friendship.

'I have worked with Gerhard Berger, Michael Andretti, Elio de Angelis, Johnny Dumfries, Satoru Nakajima and Alain, so I think it is necessary for everybody who looks into this particular matter to consider the reality: as far as team-mates are concerned, I have always got on very well with all of them except one.'

There was a time, circa 1989-1990, when we thought we'd never hear Ayrton Senna pronounce the name Prost again, referring to him only as *he* and *him*. But that lay in the bad old days, long gone as Senna moved into his mid-thirties. He'd become a businessman employing up to 100 people (importing cars and home appliances to Brazil), launching his own brand of boats and motor cycles. The brand-name? *Driven to Perfection.*

He'd become a kind of father figure to Brazilian children, feeling almost physical pain at their poverty. He invested a million dollars in an education and entertainment service for children — 'they follow what I do so I like to create something for them' — and part of that involved a magazine, *Senninha* (which translates to Little Senna) to be distributed free in schools.

When Senna chooses to wield his charm it can unbalance your equilibrium in its humble gentility

---

Calms and contradictions. Could it have been no more than three months before this chilled January day that at Suzuka, Japan, he sought out Eddie Irvine, an Irish debutant in a Jordan who'd driven (let us say) without due respect to *him*, and used a very pungent expletive six times before cuffing him? Or that he'd been given a two-race suspended ban for it?

Is this threat of the ban hanging over you?

'If you hadn't mentioned it, well, I had even forgotten about it. I don't think about it. My main objective is getting completely over that issue. My attitude is a lot more to do with the real work than to keep thinking about any political steps right now.'

Jordan are imminently expected to announce that Irvine will drive for them in 1994. Do you foresee any problems driving against him again?

'I have no idea and I am not really bothered about it at this stage.'

That afternoon Senna sits under the awning of the Rothmans motorhome with a Japanese photographer who is showing his wares, a wedge of pictures of Senna. He handles them delicately and with infi-

Getting the feel of the Williams.

nite care ('this one with the white background is nice') and the siege assumes bizarre proportions again: the photographers gather and take pictures of Senna and a photographer looking at photographs. The whole thing seems to be folding in, feeding off itself.

Later there will be time for a chat with Senna. This time he sits under the awning of the Williams motorhome, at the end of a small table, and if there's an unstated tension — his reported objection to how the British Press covered the Irvine incident at Suzuka — it never surfaces. This is partly, I assume, because he's already been asked about Irvine and dealt with that, partly because he must know that if Irvine had cuffed *him* we'd have flayed and castigated Irvine; but also because, face-to-face, he is instinctively polite. When Senna chooses to wield his charm it can unbalance your equilibrium in its humble gentility.

(In another context he'd say that 'some of the media don't really understand what it takes to drive a Formula 1 car and be successful, and some believe they are judges. We are all human beings and have our difficulties in delivering all the time. Often they criticize in a destructive sense. If it is constructive, fine, but when the goal is to destroy, that's revolting'.)

The perma-smile is wan and slow-burning now. Ayrton Senna has a disconcerting habit of facing a questioner eye-to-eye and prolonging that until the end of the answer: deep eyes which assess and penetrate rather than cut. He selects each word with laboured care and, revealingly, twice asks for a word in a question to be explained, something he doesn't ordinarily do.

Your initial impressions of the car? Is the driver in you being restrained at the moment?

'Very much, because I don't feel *within* the car yet, and also the driving position isn't the best one for me yet. It will require a change to give me more of a control over the steering. Right now I don't have a good control of it. Some of that, but not all, is down to its position. Therefore you have to be very careful.'

He spoke of motivation, the favourite word we've heard already. 'You learn and you tend to move your learning process on. I know the initial part of the season is going to be much more learning, a bigger learning process, so the motivation goes up' — not just a new team but the 1994 rule changes, a return to passive suspensions on the cars, refuelling and the rest. He insisted that in general he wasn't driving faster than in the past ('I'm not driving slower, either') but had grown wiser, handling cars and situations with more precision, making more correct decisions.

The questions and answers flowed easily forward until he said 'Hey, this was supposed to be five minutes. Look at the time!' It's been a generous half hour and the chat breaks up in good humour and handshakes and his haunting politeness. He says 'thank you' for coming when it ought to be the other way round.

The car and the rest of 1994 beckon. As he walks off towards both there it is again, the balance, the body simultaneously slack and taut, the animalism of the athlete, of Lewis and Christie, and Ali and Pele, and Eusebio who used to play just down the road. You see just such on the Savannah among hunter and prey. They too can move from the slack to the taut very, very quickly — but not at 320kph.

The official presentation of Ayrton Senna after he departed Marlboro

McLaren for Williams, replacing the retired Prost, was made in October 1993. There were fewer undercurrents than you might imagine. By nature Formula 1 activists are defensive and/or outright secretive, measuring out enough information to fill a kind of facade but rarely allowing a glimpse of what lies behind it. The presentation, in the conference centre behind the Williams factory at Didcot, proved (in the activists' context) candid and extremely amusing. Senna allowed many glimpses of his impish, waspish sense of humour — and it really didn't matter that he happened to be in Sao Paulo at the time, not Didcot.

You have to prepare yourself psychologically for the sort of mind games he can play

---

It was two presentations, in fact: Frank Williams and Damon Hill here, Senna there and a phone link-up between. Because what followed sometimes — tantalizingly — went behind the facade, I propose to allow the principals to speak entirely for themselves. What they said is of more than temporal interest.

Ayrton Senna and Damon Hill in the Championship in 1994. Perhaps you could give us your comments on that?

Frank Williams: In my opinion it's going to be the strongest driver pairing. I feel very, very confident with the two drivers. It will depend on our technology.

How long are Ayrton's and Damon's contracts?

Williams: Ayrton's is for two years. Damon we have a long contract with. We've taken up a further year of that with an option in our favour until 1995. Regarding money I can say nothing. I've seen the speculation in the press and it is speculation. (Of this, more in a moment.)

Your feelings, Damon?

Hill: Obviously I was very relieved that Frank made the decision I hoped for. It wasn't quite as anxious a wait as it was the year before, because I knew my results had gone most of the way to making up Frank's mind.

Damon, you've driven with two of the world's finest drivers, Nigel Mansell of course when you were a test driver here and this year with four times World Champion Alain Prost. Are you looking forward to driving alongside Ayrton?

Hill: I think that you have to have mixed emotions about facing the prospect of driving alongside someone of the calibre of Ayrton because he's fiercely competitive, but nevertheless I expect to learn quite a lot from being with him. It's a challenge to any racing driver. I welcome it and I'm thrilled to be able to have the opportunity. I don't really know Ayrton very well. I've spoken to him a few times but very little really. I'm looking forward to it but I'm not overawed. He is far and away the fastest driver currently around. You have to prepare yourself psychologically for the sort of mind games he can play. I'm not easily demoralized or crushed, so I'm well prepared for that. I'm still on the upward climb in my Formula 1 career. I still have a lot to learn and someone like Ayrton being in the team will only add to my experience.

Williams: I think I've heard the word reputation mentioned (by implication) twice in the last three questions. Alain Prost 12 months ago had a reputation for being very, very political and very divisive in a team, and in fact the opposite was true. Alain is one of the nicest guys I've ever worked with. I also believe that the reputation of the driver depends very much on the environment in which he is working. We've a happy team here and we intend to extend that into 1994 with Ayrton.

Frank, we were here in this room a year ago and you were understandably guarded about Damon. You hoped he might win a race. We're looking now at a situation where he won three and might have won five. Do you think he'll race Senna?

Williams: I think he'll give Ayrton a very hard time immediately, yes, and that's what we want.

Can we take it from that that both drivers will be driving for the Championship?

Williams: That is correct, yes.

Hill: Let's put that into context. It was only my first full season, so if I can start 1994 with the prospect of having a serious chance of becoming World Champion I can only say it's a tremendous opportunity which I will grab on to.

Williams: I've always wanted Ayrton to drive for Williams. He is an outstanding World Champion in terms of his greatest ambition, which is winning races and winning Championships. Negotiations happened very quickly once it became apparent that Alain was serious about racing only until the end of 1993 and not beyond. I've been talking on and off with Ayrton for 10 years. My decision to sign Ayrton had no part in Alain's decision to retire, not at all.

Hill: It's always quite sad when someone like Alain leaves the sport and I enjoyed being a team-mate with him. I found him very, very straightforward but also very committed. He seems so quiet when you meet him. I've always been aggressive but you have to learn to control it. There's a right time and a right way.

Do you consider Ayrton has been taken on as number one driver or are both men considered equal?

Williams: Clearly we're expecting greater things from Ayrton than we are of Damon, but Damon continues to surprise us every race he goes to — he surprises me more at each race than the previous one — and the opportunity is wide open for him.

That wasn't a clear answer . . .

Williams: I thought it was very charitable in every sense. I think Damon will have to push himself very, very hard to keep up with Ayrton but he's surprised me all year. I would not be surprised if he runs with him and even beats him. It could happen.

(At this point, the telephone connection is established: Senna is in Sao Paulo with Betise Assumpdao translating into Portuguese for the reporters gathered there.)

Williams: Hello. We've a lot of your friends from the European media here and I'd like to welcome you to join us on their behalf. I'll pass you over to Richard (West, team-member acting as master of ceremonies in Didcot) who has some questions for you Ayrton. Thank you. The media are listening to every word you say. OK, this is Richard for you.

West: Ayrton, it's good to speak to you again. One of the questions that has come up today. Yourself and Frank have been talking for many years. *Can you please give us your feelings about finally driving for the Williams team?*

Senna: OK. Nice to talk to you, Richard. Good afternoon to everyone there, to Frank and all the media. This is a sort of link-up again because back in 1983 Frank was the man who gave me the first opportunity in my whole career to drive a Formula 1 car. Since then

The chilled sun of Estoril in January 1994 produced a symmetry of shadows.

on a number of occasions we talked, we negotiated. It's been 10 years since then and we finally came together now. I am very happy and I'm really looking forward to driving for Williams, to drive alongside Damon. I think 1993 was a wonderful start to Damon's career and what can I say? I'm really happy.

West: I'd like, if I may, to take some questions from the floor.

Do you expect to win the Championship?

Senna: Well, that's really tough, you know, it's been so long since I won my last one that I don't remember (laughter in Didcot) but I'll give it a chance.

Were you aware of the McLaren-Peugeot engine deal before you left McLaren?

Senna: I think I shouldn't compromise anybody. I have been in close contact this year not only with Frank but Ron and my decision was very clear in the taking some time ago. It was something I believed was the best thing for me and the team. Therefore it is not really relevant, the Peugeot deal being through or not.

Are you disappointed you won't be driving with Alain Prost in 1994?

Senna: Frank, we miss you so much (a roar of laughter in Didcot).

Williams: A good answer, Ayrton.

Senna: The line suddenly goes dead, we cut off the line (more laughter).

If you hadn't secured this deal with Frank would you have taken next year off?

Senna: That was also a possibility but it quickly went away because I had a feeling that I should compete strongly in the future. My priority was to get something sorted out with Frank.

West: A continuation of that question. *Have you at any time, Ayrton, considered a future in IndyCar racing?*

Senna: Yes, last year. At the end of last year I came very close to doing so and I'm just happy that I didn't do it, that I stayed committed to Formula 1 and participated in the 1993 Championship with McLaren and therefore carried on working on my Formula 1 career, preparing myself for the future.

'. . . in some ways the past two years have been a limiting factor on different driving styles'

Do you see Damon as a serious title contender?

Senna: First of all, for obvious reasons I think without any doubt Damon today is a different driver than he was when the 1993 Championship started, or at least at the same time last year. He has now almost a full season, he has won Grands Prix, he has been on pole position and he has fought his way up in a natural way. It gives drivers a lot of confidence, which is fundamental for future success, and I believe that for next year he will be a lot more competitive right away, from the very first race — which is an important thing for the Championship. As I said earlier, he couldn't have had a better start than a first season with Alain and a second season with me, so he must be extremely motivated and faces — and faced — a tremendous challenge driving for Williams alongside Alain and myself two years in a row. He has proved he is capable of winning races, and he can only improve. It could be very interesting for him but also for me and for many English fans next year.

What effect will the new rules have?

Senna: Perhaps Formula 1 won't change as much as people expect, but it will change because some of the technology that has been banned will lead to a situation of more driver input, not only on the set-up of the car but in driving it. I believe it's the right way as far as the drivers are concerned, so we can exploit different driving styles a little bit better. I believe and I feel that in some ways the past two years have been a limiting factor on different driving styles. I hope that it will be more competitive with other teams than Williams (prominent) but I hope Williams will stay ahead and give us the ability to have a very successful season again.

(From a reporter in Sao Paulo to Frank Williams, which Betise diplomatically translates into English as: *Do you think 1994 will be as boring with Senna winning in a Williams as 1993 was with Prost winning in a Williams?*)

Senna, intervening: Actually the journalist here asked *don't you think the Championship will be even MORE boring with Senna?* (A roar of laughter in Didcot.) That's what he said, word by word (more laughter).

Williams: First point. I don't think the 1993 Championship has been boring. Second point. I think 1994 is going to be a much tougher Championship, partly because of the changes to the cars. No-one stays on top for ever. There will be some teams pushing us, maybe beating us. Quite likely.

Senna: OK, Frank. We are happy here with your words and we say goodbye for the moment, not only to you but everybody there in England and I'm looking forward to seeing you soon.

Williams: Thank you very much, Ayrton. It's very good to talk to you and I say that on behalf of everybody here. I'll speak to you later today.

Senna: Goodbye for now.

During the 1994 siege at Estoril those four months later, Senna was asked (again!) if he regretted that Prost wouldn't be driving in Formula 1 in 1994 and he replied cryptically that if Prost did emerge from retirement *it would be good for my bank balance.* Curiously nobody pursued Senna into that statement, curiously because it seemed incomprehensible. How could Prost's return — to McLaren,

as was rumoured, or anywhere else — earn money for Senna?

A strange affair, as it subsequently transpired. Williams had negotiated an exclusion clause with Prost, paying him £5.1 million not to drive for another team. If Prost did emerge from retirement he'd have to pay it back, and — as part of Senna's negotiations — he, Senna, would inherit the money.

A week after Estoril, McLaren unveiled their new car at their factory in Woking and without waiting to be asked the 'inevitable' Ron Dennis, the company's managing director, spoke. Again I reproduce this because it is of more than temporal value.

'There are two issues. The first is that the contractual relationship between Alain and his former team and sponsors is of interest to us but, of course, of no relevance. It is not our business what the situation is or was and, as far as we are concerned, he represents a driver who won three of his four World Championships in a McLaren. That inevitably makes him extremely suitable to drive for McLaren in 1994, but at this moment nothing has been decided.

'Second, people have asked me *has he a desire to drive?* and I have a simple answer to that. *I don't think that you have to pay people NOT to do things they don't want to do.* If you are being paid not to drive, logically there seems to be a desire to drive. Of course everybody is entitled to change their mind. It is a human trait. I believe that most Grand Prix drivers would actually race cars for nothing. If the economic situation prevailing at the time removed the ability to pay them to do it, well, they would do it because they like doing it, they get a tremendous buzz from beating another individual in another Grand Prix car. These are days of multi-million dollar retainers but forget that. These guys enjoy racing and enjoy driving and when it is removed from them they are given time to reflect. I think they start to re-consider the radical nature of their decision.

'There is a unique situation at McLaren because Jean-Pierre Jabouille (managing director of Peugeot Sport) and myself are very close friends of Alain's. The friendship side of McLaren is not often recognised by outsiders but it is often recognised by drivers. We are sometimes considered to be somewhat sterile, but I can assure you that when you are on the inside functioning with the team it's an

Left *The face of '94.*

39

unusual environment. I think that is something Alain missed. He didn't find it in the other teams he drove for when he left McLaren (Ferrari, Williams) and, looking to the future, it is an extremely attractive environment for him to function in. I think that is why he is thinking of returning.'

Prost won 30 times in a McLaren, Senna 35, Prost took 10 pole positions, Senna 46

An unusual day at Woking, the unveiling of the new McLaren and its Peugeot engine conducted in the trophy room, glass shelves around the walls with such ornate cups on them — cups which chart the team's triumphal days. The name of Alain Prost is engraved on a lot of them, the name of Ayrton Senna on a lot of them: Prost won 30 times in a McLaren, Senna 35, Prost took 10 pole positions, Senna 46; between them they took every Championship from 1985 to 1991 except 1987.

Unusual? A late January day, no sallow sun even, Senna gone and Prost not returned. Instinctively, like on the empty pit lane straight at Estoril, you looked for them, listened for Prost's glorious way of chewing English vowels, waited for Senna's way of stroking them. Instead the only driver McLaren did have, Mika Hakkinen, posed on and near the car — Hakkinen who'd yet to win a race, bring a trophy for the glass shelves.

This book is about what Ayrton Senna did bring.

CHAPTER THREE

The Third Championship

Sometimes when I am out jogging I say to myself you have won three World Championships. I say it in different ways. I know how good I have to be but I have absorbed it in a healthy way. It has come from hard work from me and others. It is a great achievement but achieved with a lot of logic.
— *Ayrton Senna*

THE SETTING, MOVING towards the United States Grand Prix at Phoenix on 10 March 1991, first race of the season: Nigel Mansell had been lured from retirement by Williams and testing implied he'd be strong. How strong? Gerhard Berger, who'd joined Senna at Marlboro McLaren in 1990, set himself to test and test throughout the winter in order to be fitter than Senna and more familiar with the car. Could he actually beat Senna, Senna who rested and recuperated in Brazil?

Senna had tested Honda's V12 at Estoril in late autumn and the week before Phoenix returned to Estoril to try it in McLaren's new MP4/6. With complete candour he said of the engine 'I don't know what they (Honda) have been doing since, but there is not enough progress and not enough power'. He'd add 'we developed the V12 engine last year and when I drove it in October the engine already had a good performance. There was a programme established by the

Honda engineers, some targets to be achieved in terms of reliability, output power, driveability. Now that I come back after all those months to drive the car we clearly are not there. They know it, it's not a secret. They have the figures from their test bench data. The only difference is that instead of not telling the truth I tell it'.

Consternation: no feeding of the facade. Normally drivers don't say those things, and certainly not in public. When Honda supplied Williams in 1984, for instance, the team took a policy decision never to blame the engine, however difficult that made the season: Keke Rosberg eighth and Jacques Laffite joint fourteenth in the Championship.

Moreover the widely-held perception was that the Japanese, individually or collectively, might regard open criticism of their efforts as a loss of face. Honda issued a statement which insisted that the V12 was already putting out more horsepower than the V10 and the engine they'd run at Estoril this early spring was in Phoenix-spec, unrepresentative of the kind you needed for Portugal. 'Traditionally Honda has detuned its engines for the first race of the year. We tend to go for reliability rather than power. There is a continuous development programme all through the year. It's always been planned that way. This is not a panic reaction to the comments.'

The days were ticking towards Phoenix. Senna saw the perils of a season without enough power and resolved to do some hard driving in the background, urging Honda on. It produced a rich irony. He damaged his own argument by winning Phoenix and Brazil and Imola and Monaco. It made the hard driving infinitely more difficult.

In Phoenix qualifying he decisively outperformed Berger and that climaxed during the second session. Senna 1m 21.434s. Berger 1m 23.742s — Senna pole (his fifty third), Berger seventh on the grid. This exercised a profound effect on Berger, who needed nearly half the season to recover his confidence.

Of the pole lap Senna said 'very exciting, a great feeling. I think any time in the one minute 23s would be difficult to beat, but it is important to believe you can do it and be in the right place at the right time'.

Alain Prost, who'd moved from Marlboro McLaren to Ferrari as Berger moved from Ferrari to Marlboro McLaren, lined up alongside Senna on the front row. At the green they lurched towards each

The start of the third World Championship. Senna takes the lead in Phoenix, 1991, followed by Alain Prost (Ferrari).

Like all street circuits, this one requires power and precision.

other but that was just the power coming on, slewing the cars. Both steadied, Senna already half a length clear. An instant later Prost slotted behind, the two Williamses (Riccardo Patrese in the other) lurking, Berger wide to the left searching for a gap.

This arrangement altered convulsively on the short, sharp journey to Turn One, a right. Mansell flung the Williams full left and so did Patrese, squeezing and freezing Berger. Mansell drew level with Prost but Prost fought that. In the gullies between the concrete walls Senna caressed the McLaren. He settled the race at the end of lap 1.

> Senna   lm 34.355s
> Prost   lm 36.167s
> Mansell   lm 36.647s

On the second lap Senna increased that, caressing the McLaren more urgently so that the gap to Prost stretched to 2.654s, 2.996 next lap, then 3.368, then 4.100. Prost's Ferrari seemed to buck and twitch, Mansell seemed to be hauling the Williams by the strength of his forearms, Jean Alesi, partnering Prost, hammer-hammer-hammered. Senna flowed, the concrete walls were riverbanks.

By lap 7 he lapped back-markers and after 30 laps the gap stretched to 18.475s. The race, like so many street races, took its toll: Mansell out (gearbox). Berger out (fuel pressure). Patrese out (accident). Senna crossed the line 16.322 seconds before Prost and spoke analytically, moving down the salient points — the car worked well except for a minor gearbox problem, the balance wasn't quite right which affected the steering, but 'I was able to maintain a good pace and I stopped for tyres at the right time'. Pure Senna-speak.

Two weeks later at Interlagos, Patrese held pole until the dying moments of the second session. This needs closer examination, not least because of Senna's suspicions that sooner or later the McLaren Honda would struggle against the Williams Renault. In the morning untimed session Patrese peaked on his twenty fourth and final lap, one minute 17.247s. Senna peaked on his thirty first and final lap, one minute 17.483s. Mansell covered 26 laps, peaking on the twenty second with one minute 17.094. 'When the two Williams did low 17s

Left *Mighty background, mighty foreground. Senna on his way to beating Prost by 16.322 seconds.*

45

I realised we were in for a major challenge,' Senna said.

Now the qualifying and the analytical mind. 'In my first run I got ahead of them and suddenly they improved by over half a second. I knew it was going to take two things, to change the car technically and drive to a higher level.' The first runs:

Senna   1:17.282
Mansell   1:17.356, then 1:16.843
Patrese   1:17.647, then 1:16.775

With five minutes left Prost thrust in one minute 17.739, only third row of the grid. Two minutes later Senna tried again, 'motivated enormously by the desire to succeed in front of my home crowd. The support they gave me was inspirational. When you are moving out of the pits a billion things go through your mind and body. It's an amazingly fast process, all geared to one goal, all focused to one minor point. It's something so far away that your eyes cannot see. It's really in your mind. We changed a few details to the chassis set-up between the first and second runs and I also modified my line through some of the corners. Even so, at one point on my second run I was well over the limit, riding one of the kerbs'. At the two timing points Senna reached over 300kph (186mph) for the first time. One minute 16.392. Pole.

At the green light Senna made a clean start, Mansell clinging but Patrese losing touch and the rest strung back. Only Mansell could match him and in the looping corners managed to draw up to him, couldn't pass. Mansell made an early pit stop and a slow one (14.59 seconds) as he wrestled the semi-automatic gearbox. Senna came in a lap later, a swift 6.93 seconds. Order: Senna, Patrese, Alesi, Mansell. Neither Patrese nor Alesi had stopped yet and when they did the order settled to Senna, Mansell, Piquet, Patrese, Alesi.

Mansell charged and after 29 laps cut the gap to 7.267, kept on cutting it, 4.8, 3.1. Senna responded, forced the gap out to 8.545 and Mansell pitted for more tyres after a puncture. It was lap 50, and 21 remained. Watching, you could hardly know the forces at work. Senna 'lost third and fifth gears at one point and just hooked it into sixth'.

Mansell spun furiously — gearbox — and retired. Senna trapped in sixth gear, Patrese mounted an attack, hacking the gap to 20 seconds.

Two out of two. Senna wins Brazil, limping home 2.991 seconds in front of Riccardo Patrese (Williams).

'I saw Patrese coming for me and I really didn't think I'd make it.'

	Senna	Patrese
Lap 65	1:28.305	1:21.990
Lap 66	1:28.621	1:22.320
Lap 67	1:25.899	1:21.429

That hacked the gap to 14 seconds. The camera on Senna's car told a tale. On the loops out at the back of the circuit, the lefts and rights, not once did his hand move to change gear. He tip-toed, the rain lurking in darkening folds of cloud.

	Senna	Patrese
Lap 68	1:25.781	1:21.617
Lap 69	1:24.721	1:23.433

The gap hacked down to nine seconds, down to 5.4 at lap 69.

Lap 70	1:25.177	1:24.711

That brought the gap to 4.158 and the rain was falling, a deliverance. Senna's engine rumbled and grumbled and gurgled and, into the last, the gap stood at 3.6. Senna lifted his right hand and stabbed the index finger towards the leaden sky. *Stop the race!* They didn't. He crept on, the wetness of the track prohibiting a final assault by Patrese.

Lap 71   1:28.985   1:28.284

Senna won by 2.991 seconds. 'I felt it was my duty to win in Brazil. I pushed the car regardless of the rain. I was also suffering from cramps and muscle spasms in my upper body, partly because the harness was slightly too tight, partly through emotion.'

When he crossed the line and stopped he stayed in the cockpit, helmet off, head thrown back. 'I lost the engine completely and I couldn't re-start it. Then the pain was unbelievable. I tried to relax. I had such a huge pain in my shoulders and in my side I didn't know whether I should shout, cry or smile. I just didn't know what was going on.'

Senna responding emotionally to the emotion of a Brazilian crowd is obvious for all the obvious reasons plus one. He is intensely patriotic. ('My perfect day is to wake up at home in Brazil, at the farm or my beach house, with my family and friends: then go to a circuit

Three out of three. Senna wins San Marino – having taken Patrese for the lead.

anywhere in the world and be transported back home that evening.')

A few days after Sao Paulo. Senna tested at Imola, Betise Assumpdao there to relay his thoughts to the assorted media who have a voracious daily appetite. Since Betise is very much Brazilian herself I asked her about what you might call the Brazilian context.

'Like any other Latin country, you're really good when you're cool. There's an advertisement for cigarettes with Gerson, the 1970 World Cup footballer, and the translation of the slogan would be *You have to get the most out of everything*. To a Brazilian that means taking advantage, although in a good way. That's the cool way to be: take advantage of everything you possibly can in life, try to fool everybody, be smarter than them, shrewder. On the beach you adopt the laid-back way, take the mickey out of everybody and then there's sex and all that. Of course it's a macho thing. Senna is not that at all.

'Another thing. We say OK, see you at seven o'clock but everybody knows you won't. What to the Anglo-Saxons is five minutes is half an hour to Brazilians. If you arrive at the right time they'll say *what are you doing here? I haven't even had my shower yet!* Senna is not like that at all. In fact he is exactly the opposite. He makes a point of being punctual, of doing everything he has to do in the right way. If he's late it's because he's been held up.

'Brazilians are supposed — in the eyes of other people — to laugh and be happy the whole time. Senna is not like that. It's not that he doesn't want people to like him, it's that he is not going to change the way he is just so that people will like him. The people have always liked him, but what is peculiar (in Brazil) is that a guy like Senna should be a hero. People go mad.

'When he went to his house in Sao Paulo after the Grand Prix there were 2,000 people in front of it. He couldn't get through and had to get into a police car to reach the house. The crowd stayed until one o'clock in the morning and the police asked Ayrton to come out. Otherwise the 2,000 would never have gone and the police began to fear there were bound to be some problems.

'Senna had to come out and stand on top of the three-metre wall with the trophy so that everybody could see him again, on the understanding that once they had seen him they'd disperse. It's peculiar that the people like him the way they do, although of course he gets results.'

Some cameos from that Imola testing. A long-limbed girl, lycra

Four out of four. Senna wins Monaco, beating Nigel Mansell (Williams) by 18.348 seconds.

stockings which go all the way up the limbs, wears a mini skirt not much longer than a bikini. She positions herself as near to the McLaren pit as she can get and insists she's come from Milan because she's an old friend of Ayrton, popped along to say hello. Her patience is rewarded. If he doesn't recognise her, he has the art of suggesting he does. They chat briefly while the photographers gorge. He smiles and she's thrilled. Is it — on her behalf — a publicity stunt? Has she hired one of the photographers? Has a photographer hired her? Who knows? To Senna: just another moment in just another test session.

The crowd here at Imola, and testing at Imola invariably attracts a crowd, transmit the opposite of Latin warmth to Senna. Whenever he takes the McLaren out to combat the times Prost is setting in the Ferrari they jeer and taunt.

The sense of siege lay hard here. The McLaren motorhome, parked at the rear of the paddock some 30 or 40 yards from the pit, had a smoked-glass upper deck. Senna inhabited that. He didn't stray down to the cluster of tables in a cordoned off area along the flank of the motorhome. To reach the pit he emerged very suddenly, walked briskly across the paddock into a narrow valley between the transporters, passed into the bowels of the pit and instantaneously a mechanic drew a rope over the back of the pit. Senna inhabited the pit, sometimes almost in shadow. From time to time people called his name, a TV crew loomed, the long-limbed lady lingered. After his last run he raked over this and that with the engineers, emerged from the pit very suddenly and walked briskly towards the motorhome. The TV crew struggled to keep up with him — *Ayrton, Ayrton* — and he disappeared into the smoked-glass upper-deck, refuge from the siege.

I often wonder what cumulative effect this has on human beings if it is replicated everywhere that human being goes. Apply that to your bank manager. Suppose he emerges to have lunch and finds several hundred people jostling to be near him, a loose-limbed lady insisting she's a friend, a TV crew bawling his name; same at lunch and on the way back; same when he finishes work; and when he reaches home 2,000 people are camped round his house and he needs a police car to get in. Now multiply this day by day for the major part of a decade . . .

At Imola, Senna seemed more than usually preoccupied, sometimes de-briefing until past 10 in the evening. Betise explained it. 'He's trying to analyse the information the computer gives out. Now they have computers for everything, all the aerodynamics, suspension, everything — and to take an example, it gives the suspension performance in every corner. If you can't read it properly, you don't know what's happening and you can't use what the computer is saying to the full capacity. Senna wants to know everything. People show him graphics and the other day he said 'Is that good? Is that supposed to be good? Is that what it's supposed to be?' He is spending more time now in the briefings because he wants to analyse, to understand. You know what he's like. The engineers give him information but he wants to know why he goes up here and down there.'

A couple of weeks later he took pole for the San Marino Grand Prix and a wet race conjuring a freakish parade lap. Prost hit a rivulet of water and floated off onto a grassy incline, where the Ferrari stuck. Berger also floated off but at a slightly different angle. He was able to use the incline to regain the track. Prost clambered from the Ferrari, his race ended before it had begun. This does not make you popular at Imola.

Green light. For a fraction of a second Senna seemed to have made the better start but Patrese, abreast, slithered and twitched round the outside of the corner called Tamburello.

Senna tucked in behind, Patrese flinging spray from puddles so deep they reflected the overhanging trees. Senna retreated on the straights to lessen the spray, drew up at the corners. On that opening lap Mansell went out, tapped by Martin Brundle's Brabham. Senna retreated further. His thinking: *We had to run a compromise setting because we knew the track would dry. Patrese made a better start. I waited behind him until the track conditions improved.*

Ending lap 9 Senna advanced and, in the complex before the pit lane straight, tucked inside, took the racing line and the lead. Patrese immediately pitted for slick tyres but, stationary, the engine wouldn't fire. Senna led Berger by five seconds, Berger catching him, they waded into back-markers. A problem: the dry line was very dry but no more than the width of a car. Dare Senna step off it to overtake, risk his slick tyres on the wet? Dare Berger? Senna did and had three back-markers like a shield between himself and Berger.

Who bothered about Patrese simply giving the Williams a run, Patrese who'd lost four laps in the pits? Senna cut past him and cut past a back-marker thinking *well, I won't be seeing Patrese again for a while.* Senna accelerated from the back-marker. In short order Patrese took the back-marker and re-caught Senna and set fastest lap.

Senna did not miss the significance. His thinking: *If the Williams is capable of that, what happens when it goes a full race distance?* No matter that soon enough Patrese was wandering round, the engine gone. The point had been made, underscored by two facts: this season a win counted 10 points and all 16 races counted. With 13 after Imola it left 130 points for the taking, a potential mountain if the Williams Renault came good. (Renault, applying vast funds and resources to their engines, regarded themselves as crusaders proving to European manufacturers that the Japanese could be beaten.)

Senna won Imola from Berger. 'Halfway through, my oil pressure dropped and the warning light came on and I thought I wouldn't finish so I slowed until Gerhard started to catch me.' Three wins out of three, Senna hard-driving in the background but — *Ayrton, you've won the three out of three, what's the fuss you're making about?*

Qualifying at Monaco produced a feat by Stefano Modena, who

Mighty background, troubled foreground. He went as far as lap 25 in Canada and the electrics failed.

Pastoral background, troubled foreground. He crashed in practice at the fearsome Peralta corner and finished the Mexican GP a distant third.

put his Tyrrell onto the front row beside Senna, Patrese and Piquet on the second. Mansell and Berger on the third. (Insight from Brundle: 'Senna takes difficult conditions and circuits in his stride. Some of his qualifying laps and his wins at Monte Carlo, for instance, have been absolutely breathtaking. I know how hard it is there. You have to be so precise and have such self-belief to be quick there and he is. He excels at Monaco and it's brilliant to watch'.)

Senna led into Ste Devote but as the race developed Modena hung and clung. Senna gave his familiar performance in the traffic, butchering it, while Modena spent fruitless, frustrating laps captive of it. That put Senna more than 20 seconds ahead. Modena's engine blew, spewing oil onto the track. Patrese, close, couldn't miss it and spun, battering the Williams. Senna eased off, Prost was a distant second but Mansell — an engine misfire correcting itself — moved in on Prost. Out of the tunnel Mansell went fast, on the incline to the chicane he went fast and into the chicane wedged and bustled through on nerve, on verve.

Senna glimpsed this on a vast television screen in the pits. His thinking: *Well, what does await me when the Williams Renault goes a full race distance?* Subsequently Senna glanced up at the screen and saw Last Lap on it, although he thought there ought to be two more. 'I kept going, got to the finishing line after another lap and Jacky Ickx gave me the chequered flag. I slowed down for about half a lap and then Ron Dennis called me on the radio telling me to speed up because there was another lap to go! I'd already undone my seat belts but I did what he said. Monte Carlo is very hard physically because it's bumpy and it hurts a lot, your shoulders, your neck and so on. It really hurts (smile) but I won and I'm happy.' And four out of four, too. No man had taken the first four of a season before. Senna 40, Prost 11, Berger 10, Patrese and Mansell 6.

Canada changed it. Patrese took pole from Mansell, Senna third. 'As usual I tried my hardest today, but two people managed to do better and deserved to be up in front. Until now people think we have had it easy with four pole positions and four wins, but my performance shows how competitive it is out there.' The meaning: *we have to do better.*

The power balance of the season shifted, Mansell leading from

Patrese, Senna third but melting from them until the electrics failed. 'Honestly I don't think I could have beaten the two Williams.' Mansell ought to have won but, in sight of the finishing line, the car failed giving the race to Piquet, Modena second and Patrese third.

Senna arrived in Mexico after a crash on a jet ski. He fell off one and another, coming up behind, hit him. He needed 10 stitches in his head. Professor Sid Watkins, the Formula 1 doctor, pronounced him fit and, with five minutes of the first qualifying session left, he tried to take provisional pole from Patrese. He reached the corner called Peralta, an uneven broad sweep of a right which Senna judged was no longer safe.

Coming from the left-hander towards Peralta he positioned the McLaren to the outside, creating space to select the optimum line. He turned in, riding mid-track, turned further. As the sweep of Peralta embraced him the McLaren bucked and slewed to the outside, revolving crazily. It skittered off backwards, battered a tyre wall broadside, rose and revolved, flipped, landed upside down. 'Up to

By France the two Williams with their Renault power were proving hard to hold. Senna finished third.

that point the car was going quite well but my fifth gear was too short and I was changing to sixth with one hand on the wheel when I hit a bump and lost it.'

Rain fell in second qualifying so the Friday times stood. Patrese, Mansell, Senna.

Mexico has a cavernous straight from the grid, an aeroplane runway of a straight inviting jostling and jockeying and proper jousting. When the cavalcade of cars reached Turn One from the green light, Mansell led from Alesi, Senna third, Patrese fourth, Berger fifth. Crossing the line to complete lap 1 Alesi and Senna moved like nervous fish: Senna darted hard right and drew alongside Alesi, who didn't appreciate that. They nearly rubbed gills. Senna darted full left for Turn One. Alesi darted towards him, Senna covered it by darting to mid-track. Alesi nosed out, looking and searching but too late. Senna, decisively ahead, had a clear run at Mansell and within the next few laps got more confirmation.

	Mansell	Senna
Lap 2	1:25.168	1:25.334
Lap 3	1:23.815	1:23.537
Lap 4	1:23.488	1:23.600
Lap 5	1:22.359	1:22.856

These fractional differences accumulate and, worse, Patrese caught Senna and pressured him. Both the Williams cars looked nimble, Patrese so nimble that beginning lap 11 he took Senna.

	Patrese	Senna
Lap 11	1:21.128	1:23.032
Lap 12	1:23.523	1:22.515
Lap 13	1:22.407	1:23.161

Patrese flowed into the distance, Senna falling towards Piquet. Patrese took Mansell and at 21 laps led by 7.254 seconds, Senna at 10.346, Piquet at 10.905. Mansell's engine overheated, slowing him on the straight. On lap 30 Senna drew up and had a go out of Turn One. Mansell did not appreciate that. He adjusted the fuel mixture and set fastest lap, shedding Senna in the process. Mansell rapped out fastest lap, and another, and another, might have been ramming in the confirmation.

You couldn't expect to hold Mansell at Silverstone and Senna didn't. He ran out of fuel but was classified fourth.

Mansell mania packed Silverstone but at this moment every eye is on Senna.

	Patrese	*Mansell*	*Senna*
Lap 55	1:18.850	1:17.444	1:18.876
Lap 56	1:18.351	1:17.379	1:19.969
Lap 57	1:18.561	1:18.070	1:18.689
Lap 58	1:18.242	1:17.113	1:19.239

Patrese won from Mansell. Senna third at 57.356 seconds. 'The Williams were very fast and it was very hard for me to keep up the same rhythm. Honda are working hard to get more power from our engine. I couldn't get too close to the cars in front because my temperatures were very marginal. Nigel made it very hard for me, but it was a great race and this result shows that the Championship is very open. The main thing was to finish on the podium, to have four points for the Championship. That is very important at this stage and, in the meantime, to gain time to give Honda and McLaren the ability to make some corrections to the chassis and the engine particularly. About the race there's nothing to say, Riccardo dominant, Nigel quick in the later stages. They have established the level of performance that they can achieve.' Senna 44, Patrese 20, Piquet 16, Mansell 13.

At Magny-Cours, a new circuit for the French Grand Prix, Senna took provisional pole on the Friday but on the Saturday dropped to third behind Patrese and . . . Prost. Mansell fourth. 'The car and engine ran fine *but not quickly enough.*'

Senna made a self-confessed 'poor start' although many would have been pleased with it, third behind Prost and Mansell. The first lap became the matrix: Prost surging, Mansell pursuing, Senna already conceding distance. His thinking: *I knew I could not go with them. We know we do not have the engine or chassis to match the Williams and the Ferrari at the moment.* Mansell won from Prost, Senna third, half a minute adrift. 'The third place adds to my total, of course, and keeps us in the running while the technicians are working on improvements to the car.' Senna 48, Mansell 23, Patrese 22, Prost 17.

A 'new' Silverstone for the British Grand Prix, the circuit heavily doctored with a 'complex' approaching the start-finish line, a 'complex' (well, almost) at Stowe. Mansell took pole from Senna,

Main picture *Allan McNish, F3000 racer and McLaren test driver.*

Inset *The young Scotsman impressed everyone but it's not easy trying to emulate Senna and McNish's career faltered.*

Senna took a momentary lead in the race but along Hangar Straight Mansell wrung the Renault engine and could not be resisted. The Williams held an immense advantage and Mansell exploited it. Senna slogged on ('I planned to run without a tyre stop and this plan was paying off but towards the end my left front blistered, causing a slight vibration. It wasn't a problem.') He held second until the final lap when he slowed and stopped, no more fuel. On the slowing-down lap Mansell drew up and offered Senna a lift to the pits. Senna climbed aboard and tapped Mansell playfully a couple of times on the helmet. *I'm ready to go now, chauffeur.* It created one of the most evocative images of the season. Senna, classified fourth, moved to 51, Mansell 33, Patrese 22, Prost 21.

'. . . as at Silverstone, we are just not quick enough to compete with the Williams'

A week before the German Grand Prix, Senna tested at Hockenheim and crashed in the first chicane at some 300kph (186mph). Evidently a rear tyre blew, the McLaren pitched 15 feet into the air, vaulting savagely. He told fellow driver Mauricio Gugelmin he feared a direct impact with the tyre wall and twisted the car away, running onto the kerbing sideways. He hurt his neck and shoulder but recovered to compete in the Grand Prix. Fourth in first qualifying he pursued the theme. 'We have no real problems except, as at Silverstone, we are just not quick enough to compete with the Williams.' In second qualifying he produced one minute 37.274 to share the front row with Mansell. 'Maybe I could have gone one-tenth quicker but I was really on the limit . . .'

Before the race, the theme again. 'I have to be honest. We haven't had much progress since Imola, both on the engine and the car, despite some efforts which have been made.' The race? A loop of a film you'd seen before, Mansell wringing the Renault engine. Berger nipping ahead of Senna, Prost harrying Senna, Patrese beginning to harry Prost. In time, Mansell leading, Patrese wrung his Renault engine and moved up to second, leaving Senna and Prost locked into a straight fight for third. Senna versus Prost. Another loop from a film you'd seen before, reared from the past and riven with the past, of crashes and disputes and distrust.

Prost came strong, eased, calculated. Eight laps remained. Prost came strong again into Senna's slipstream and they travelled together into a gentle right curve, together down a straight, together into the next gentle right curve towards the mouth of the chicane. Prost went left. Senna covered that. Prost went further left, abreast now but the mouth of the chicane yawned into a tight right clamp.

Senna moved from mid track further across and a vice tightened on Prost as the chicane tightened towards him: he had two wheels on the edge of the track. Senna flicked clear and on to the racing line, Prost hemmed, nowhere to go except the escape road. Little plumes of smoke rose from Prost's tyres as he dipped the brake pedal. He struck a cone — an ordinary traffic cone — guarding the escape road entrance and the Ferrari chewed it. Prost parked and got out.

Senna held fourth until the last lap when he ran out of fuel again. It enraged him; Prost enraged, too, claimed Senna had blocked him unacceptably and 'then drove across me, braking in a strange way, weaving'. If, Prost added, this happens again 'I'll just have to push him off'. The past became the present.

'I think everyone knows Prost by now,' Senna said. 'He is always complaining about the car or the tyres or the team or the mechanics or the other drivers or the circuit. It's always somebody else to blame. It's never his fault. He overshot under braking, he risked a lot there, he could have put himself into an accident and also involved me in that. Fortunately we didn't touch but he almost cost me an accident and almost cost himself an accident too.'

'If I find him the same way again I push him out, that's for sure,' Prost said, 'because I can't accept that FISA give Gugelmin or (Aguri) Suzuki a 10,000 dollar fine at Magny-Cours and Silverstone and they never do anything for top drivers. If you have a rule it must be the same for everybody.' Senna 51, Mansell 43, Patrese 28, Prost 21.

In Hungary Prost and Senna made up amid chaotic scenes. They went to the Elf motorhome to watch a video of Hockenheim and emerged into a scrummage of photographers, a scrummage of such intensity it would have done credit to the straight in Mexico after the green light, jostling and jousting. Prost, speaking softly, said it was time to bury the past and safeguard the future. Would that last? Could it last? Nobody knew.

Senna constructed a beautiful race to win Hungary, tilting the Championship towards himself.

Senna took pole from Patrese and Mansell and, whimsical (as he can be) offered these words. 'This has been the longest time in the last few years that I have been off the pole position so it feels very good. When you experience something good you get used to it! The pole position is the result of the team's improvement and not because others have had problems.'

He made his two runs in the Saturday session, warming to 1:16.684, warming to 1:16.147 which stood in direct comparison to Patrese's 1:17.379 and Mansell's 1:17.389. After the session Senna came up to the Press Room for the mandatory conference and as he passed I couldn't help applauding, one of those instinctive reactions you have when you've witnessed something extraordinary.

A British journalist who'd barely seen motor racing before, inevitably doing a feature on Mansell, watched the qualifying with no more than passing interest. He emitted murmurs of appreciation as Senna created the 1:16.147, something remarkable since over the 2.466 miles (3.968km) Senna gained the merest fractions over Patrese and Mansell. It's a paradox because in full flood Senna does not radiate raw speed. He doesn't bounce the kerbing more than necessary, doesn't look as if he'd vanish over the edge of the possible, which is surely how an untutored eye would sense speed. What he does radiate is presence.

Senna created the race of a craftsman, taking Turn One round the outside of Patrese. His thinking: *Riccardo and I were on the limit but I had to go for it because leading at the first corner is crucial. My tyre choice was a calculated risk (C's left. D's right) and after two laps I thought I had a puncture. The team told me they were ready for me to come in but I tried one more lap and the problem disappeared. The car was very good out of the corner onto the main straight enabling me to control the race from the front.* Mansell moved past Patrese and finished 4.599 seconds behind Senna. It shifted the Championship again, away from the Williams now. Senna 61, Mansell 49, Patrese 32.

Senna took pole again at Spa, underlining that McLaren and Honda were back on the pace. A tumult of a Grand Prix. Prost challenging Senna heavily for the lead at the La Source hairpin. Mansell attacking Prost into Les Combes and taking him on lap 2. Prost's engine blew. Mansell caught Senna but Senna held him. Senna pitted for tyres but was stationary for 9.87 seconds, Mansell pitted next lap but was stationary only for 7.40. Order: Mansell, Alesi, Senna. Mansell went out after 22 laps, electrics. Senna's thinking: *I knew Alesi was running B compound tyres (to try and go the distance without stopping) and I decided to wait. As I pulled onto his tail coming out of the hairpin I went to change into fourth and I had a major problem with the lever, similar to Brazil. I managed to get sixth and found them all from third upwards so I never tried to go slower than this again.* Alesi pressed the lead to more than 10 seconds.

The tumult endured: Piquet tracked Senna, Patrese took Piquet, de Cesaris fifth. Alesi's engine let go on lap 30, giving Senna the lead. Patrese made a mistake, letting Piquet through and de Cesaris through and de Cesaris challenged Piquet, took him.

Patrese re-took Piquet and Berger took Piquet, too. Could de Cesaris in the Jordan overhaul a mighty McLaren Honda with Ayrton Senna driving it? A colossal question and a stark answer. No. With four laps left the Jordan's engine let go. Patrese drifted, gearbox, and Berger came in 1.901 seconds after Senna. The Championship shifted further. Senna 71, Mansell 49, Patrese 34, Berger 28.

At Monza, Senna took a third consecutive pole. 'At the start of my

*A tumult of a Belgian Grand Prix at Spa, which Senna won from Gerhard
Berger. Now look, Gerhard, this is what happened.*

second quick lap I heard over the radio about Mansell's best time' — slower. 'I knew it was just between me and Gerhard. I had to lift off at the second Lesmo because Nigel was there and though he got off the racing line I didn't want to take the risk. That cost me two-tenths of a second.'

Mansell needed to finish in front of Senna to retain hopes of the Championship. Senna led and Mansell found Patrese laying pressure on him. Mansell waved Patrese through. Mansell's thinking: *Patrese is Italian, this is Monza. Patrese is bound to go for Senna and push him, push Senna's tyres a lot more than Senna wants.*

Patrese tried lustily, boring the snout of the Williams towards Senna and had him, but at the Ascari chicane Patrese's gearbox hesitated and he spun. Senna led, Mansell clamouring over him and Senna in trouble. 'My set-up was not so good. I used up my tyres and lost grip, then my left front began to vibrate and locked under braking. Soon after, Mansell passed me and I decided to stop for fresh rubber.'

Senna returned and dispatched Schumacher, Berger and Prost — done with proper propriety by both parties, Prost hugging the left, Senna safe through the opening — although there would be no catching Mansell. Senna 77, Mansell 59, Patrese 34. Senna's thinking, rationing the mental exercise which the Championship had become: *The Williams had to win and second place has reduced our future problems, it's better than nothing. Every race adds more pressure to them. They cannot afford NOT to finish.*

Senna reinforced that before the Portuguese Grand Prix at Estoril. *I am 'pacing' my decisions more carefully because of my points lead although there are four races to go (here, Spain, Japan and Australia) and that's enough to make a radical difference. The Williams have nothing to lose so they're going for everything.*

An alarming start: Patrese fast, Mansell bursting from behind Berger, casting the Williams into Senna's path, forcing a knee-jerk reaction. Senna had to swivel to safety. 'Nigel steered his car towards mine, I must admit I let him through too easily. If this had happened at any other race I would have let the accident happen. I braked too hard at the first corner to avoid him and even so nearly lost the nosecone. I think Nigel chose the wrong strategy for the start. Nothing happened this time but next time I don't know . . .'

The relationship between Senna and Mansell is hard to quantify. It seemed to lurch from mutual self-interest to mutual self-respect to mutual hostility, seemed to oscillate and could be any of the three positions as events demanded. They'd sit (as we shall see) in a mutual communion of thought, backslapping, hand-shaking, nodding as the other spoke. They'd drive (as we shall see) with a vein of ruthlessness which had to damage the one or the other, and excercise their respective vocabularies in the aftermath. This was a marriage of inconvenience, with all that implies.

Mansell sat in the cockpit beating his fists on the steering wheel in frustration

---

Of Estoril, Berger would say 'Nigel took a big risk. I mean, I don't think it was the right way to approach it because if I had not opened the door there might have been a big crash'. Order: Patrese, Mansell, Berger, Senna. Mansell moved past Patrese and on lap 18 came in for tyres. Essentially it decided the Championship — shifted it all but finitely. It's the sort of thing you remember on a chilly January day years later when you're standing at the place where it happened and the emptiness echoes: a bare strip of concrete, nothing more.

The nut on the right rear wheel cross-threaded and the crew on it were trying to communicate that but their signals were taken to mean *all's well*. Mansell launched himself without the nut, the wheel rotated clean off and bounded into the Tyrrell pit. Mansell sat in the cockpit beating his fists on the steering wheel in frustration. The Williams team had to scamper to Mansell with a fresh wheel and fit it in the pit lane, even though it breached regulations. Mansell launched himself and from seventeenth jabbed out fastest laps. Senna's thinking: *Once I saw Patrese in the lead I pushed hard to see if he had any problems but I had to drive over the limits of myself and my car.*

Mansell pounded to eighth, kept on pounding and reached sixth before the black flag was hung, sinister as a matador's cape, the white figure 5 clear: Punishment for the work in the pit lane. Mansell cruised gently in, clambered out shoulders bowed and stalked off too upset to speak. Senna rode to second place. Senna 83, Mansell 59, Patrese 44.

The knot tightened in Spain — Berger pole from Mansell, Senna and Patrese on the second row — during the drivers' briefing which

resembled, according to one team manager, 'a kindergarten full of millionaires'. Reports of what took place in that private meeting are necessarily secondhand but:

Berger reportedly tapped Mansell playfully on the ankle (he'd sprained it playing in a Press versus Drivers football match) and Mansell reacted with vehemence.

Jean-Marie Balestre, President of FISA, addressed the drivers on the subject of the conduct at Turn One in Estoril. Balestre named no-one but said that any repetition would incur consequences.

Mansell took this personally and, the anger in the room rising, said plaintively that if he was involved in such 'incidents' it always seemed to be raised, but if Senna was involved it wasn't.

Senna took this personally and invited Balestre to have a close look at film of all the races over the past couple of years and see how many 'incidents' Mansell had been involved in. Senna also used naughty words to describe Mansell.

Piquet said he'd heard many, many years of this jaw-jaw but the war-war seemed always to remain . . .

Spain was a damp race. Berger led, with Mansell challenging Senna starkly, wheel-to-wheel, man-to-man, nerve-to-nerve, willpower-to-willpower. They veered together at the end of the long straight, neither ceding, and it seemed a terrible suction brought them closer, closer, closer. At one instant their wheels were millimetres apart. 'That was man's stuff,' Frank Williams says. 'I wish every circuit had somewhere like that . . .'

They changed wet tyres for slicks and Mansell had a slow stop. Order: Senna, Berger, Mansell. Light rain fell and Senna allowed Berger into the lead. His thinking *Mansell has to win and if I hold him up while Berger escapes into the distance, well and good.*

On lap 13 Senna spun, Mansell just missing him — a dire close-your-eyes millisecond, Senna slithering broadside across the Williams. Senna dropped to sixth and, while Mansell churned out the laps in the lead, he finished fifth. 'It was tough on us, probably

Main picture *The trick was to keep picking up points. In Portugal Berger ran third, Senna fourth – but Berger dropped out and Senna came second.*

Inset *Moving towards second place at Monza, and the chicane looks very tight from this angle.*

Left *Fifth place in Spain, but he led Mansell 85–69 in the Championship and only Japan and Australia to go.*

the hardest race of the season in terms of results. I spun because I feel the slicks we fitted to the left-hand wheels were too hard and I was fighting for grip in the wet. After the spin the left-hand tyres were blistered, making life even more difficult. Unfortunately with this problem I couldn't go quickly and climb back.' Senna 85, Mansell 69, Patrese 48. 'I am still in the stronger position.'

The position strengthened in qualifying in Japan. On the first day Berger took provisional pole from Senna and they maintained that in the second session. Senna said 'chassis balance will be crucial and the best-balanced car will emerge the winner. As far as the World Championship is concerned I feel good but I am under no illusions. The race is going to be very tough, although I think things are slowly coming our way step by step. I hope it will be the last of those steps'.

That evening Ron Dennis, Senna and Berger worked on a plan to capitalize on their grid positions, an obvious tactic but extremely effective. If you watched the start and the opening two or three laps you'd have deduced it. Green light. Berger sets off occupying the left side of the track. Senna nearly up with him and occupying the right: a wall of McLarens. They rounded Turn One in order Berger, Senna, Mansell — then through the wriggling corners towards the cross-over Berger stole clear, Senna hemming Mansell. That was the plan. And Mansell *had* to win the race.

	Berger	*Senna*	*Mansell*
Lap 1	1:46.696	1:49.924	1:50.523
Lap 2	1:45.147	1:46.304	1:46.325
Lap 3	1:44.935	1:46.014	1:46.636
Lap 4	1:45.409	1:46.578	1.45.642

That gave Berger a lead of six and a half seconds, Senna hemming Mansell, Patrese circling fourth and poised to help Mansell if he could. 'The biggest problem,' Berger said, 'was giving the tyres too hard a time in the beginning. I wanted to get as far away as possible.'

Mansell radioed the pits. *Don't panic. I'm biding my time.* There was time for that but not perhaps too much time, Berger would soon be out of reach.

	Berger	Senna	Mansell
Lap 5	1:44.582	1:45.903	1:46.273
Lap 6	1:45.824	1:46.143	1:46.106
Lap 7	1:45.265	1:45.917	1:46.192

Mansell drew back from the bounce-suck-bounce air in Senna's slip-stream. Senna knew Mansell was 'having a hell of a time in the turbulence behind me'. How long could Mansell wait, the fractions building remorselessly from Berger via Senna to himself? It was time to move back onto Senna.

	Berger	Senna	Mansell
Lap 8	1:45.855	1:46.209	1:45.783
Lap 9	1:44.872	1:46.093	1:45.941

That brought Mansell up and he radioed *preparing to attack*. They crossed the line to begin lap 10, feeling for position along the start-finish straight to the right-handed Turn One. No attack here, not possible. They twisted into Turn One, Mansell on the most normal line. Without warning the car jumped wide, careered with two wheels on the kerbing, crossed the kerbing and churned the grey-gravel run-off area. The car came to rest near the tyre wall, the Championship over.

Senna saw it. 'I cannot say I was sorry.'

'In the morning warm-up,' Mansell explained, 'I had a brake problem. We thought we'd fixed it. Unfortunately when I went into the corner the pedal went soft. I went deep because the car was very quick and very stable round there. When I put the brakes on I was caught by surprise. I wasn't slowing. I tried to make the corner and ran out of road.'

Senna thought he and Berger ought to enjoy themselves in a domestic competition and chased. The catching of Berger wouldn't take long. 'When I heard over the radio *Mansell out* I slowed to take care of the engine. Ayrton was pushing and then I thought maybe he wants to make a nice race.' Ayrton did. On lap 18 he rushed through. His thinking: *After Mansell retired it was almost an instant reaction for me to think 'right, we've got to go for it' and we can have some fun — but over the radio the team reminded me to think of the Constructors' Championship.*

Meanwhile, Berger heard a 'big engine noise and I thought *over* but the engine kept running'. Senna led. Berger followed.

Riding the big wheel in Japan.

Late in the race Senna confronted a dilemma. 'After our tyre stops I was having to drive 99.9 per cent and we had agreed earlier that whoever led for the opening stages would be allowed to win.' Senna hesitated to radio Dennis for confirmation because to voluntarily surrender any victory violated his nature, the whole purpose of his life.

'Eventually I asked the question but I couldn't hear the reply clearly over the radio and I knew nobody would believe me if I didn't give way' — (revealing how Senna views other people's view of him). 'I backed right off to reduce the engine noise and asked again. Ron said yes, he wanted us to change positions. It hurt to do it but the pain was nothing compared with the feeling from a Third World Championship. It was a small gesture to Gerhard who helped me a lot in the past, and I mean a small gesture because he was as fast as me in the race.'

Senna demonstratively slowed at the very end and two views exist about that:

1. He did it in such a way that everyone would know he could have won the Japanese Grand Prix if he had wished to win it.
2. He did it in such a way that everyone would know he valued the friendship of Berger and none could mistake the thank you.

Berger muttered cryptically 'Ayrton, I am happy to say, was thinking about me as much as I was thinking about him'.

Senna now took the opportunity to deliver two broadsides against Balestre and the infamous events of Suzuka 1989 when Senna tangled with Prost at the chicane and was disqualified, and 1990 when he'd crashed with Prost at Turn One. Senna sanitized his remarks for the television interview, although he was pungent enough.

'It has been the most competitive World Championship that I have ever competed in. Because we fought with different cars, different engines, different drivers and not inside the same team (Senna and Prost, both McLaren, dominating 1988, 1989) it was really tough. We started the year well and then we had a tough time from the fourth race onwards and, as you all know, it was a result of a lot of push from myself, from Gerhard to the team, to McLaren and to Honda and to Shell that we managed to get steps forward time after time, bit by bit, and we caught the Williams Renaults.

'Slowly we got closer to them, put pressure on them, won a couple

After Mansell crashed out – and the Championship was won – Senna gave victory to Berger, who drove strongly all through the race.

of races at the critical part of the Championship in Hungary and Belgium, scored the right results when we couldn't compete with the Williams at all. When it came really to the time, we were able to do one and two, fantastic. Therefore it's been a memorable Championship, not only for me but I think in Formula 1 terms over the last few years. The year 1989 had a disgraceful end when I won the race and it was taken away. I was prevented from going to the podium — I was just about to go to it — by Balestre and I never forget that (waves finger for emphasis). The result of that was the 1990 Championship when we fought all the way, myself and Prost, and we came to the last race and pole position was set up in the wrong place.

'We agreed before the start of qualifying with the officials that pole position would be on the outside.' (Pole should bestow a clear advantage but, if the surface of the track is dirty in the area surrounding it, that might negate the advantage.) 'Then after qualifying Balestre gave the order not to change and I found myself on the wrong side on pole. I was so frustrated I promised myself that if, after the start, I lost first place I would go for it in the first corner regardless of the result. I would go for it and Prost wouldn't turn into the first corner ahead of me and that's what took place and that was a result of the politicians making stupid decisions and bad decisions. This year what happened?

'We fought all the way, myself, Nigel, Riccardo, and when we got to the end it was only myself and Mansell. We had a hard time the last two races (Portugal, Spain). I think Mansell pushed a little over the limit but I was able to compensate for it and avoid incidents and a bad final for the Championship. In this race I was prepared to do my very best to fight for it. I was going to drive hard but I was still going to try to avoid any incidents.

'First corner, everything under control, nobody tried anything silly, Nigel was working properly, he was not going crazy, nothing happened. It was a good race, it was a competitive race I fought with Gerhard later, we were fighting each other all the time. It was a great race, exciting for everyone and, as I said, I hope this will stand as an example for myself and everyone who is competing now and the people who are coming in the future.'

At the Press Conference for journalists, Senna used much less restrained language. '1989 was unforgiveable. I still struggle to cope with that. I had a bad time with Balestre. You all know what took place here. They decided against me and that was not justice, so what took place over that winter was (expletive).

'In 1990, before we started qualifying, Gerhard and I went to the officials and asked them to change the pole position because it was in the wrong place. The officials said yes, no problem. I got pole and then what happened? Balestre gave an order that we don't change pole. We said that it had been agreed. They said no, we don't think so. That was really (expletive).

'I said to myself "OK, you try to work cleanly and do the job properly and then you get (expletived) by certain people. All right, if tomorrow Prost beats me off the line, at the first corner I will go for it and he better not turn in because he is not going to make it". And it just happened. I wish it hadn't. We were both off and it was an (expletive) end to the World Championship, it was not good for me and not good for Formula 1. It was the result of the wrong decisions and partiality from the people making them. I won the Championship. So what? It was a bad example for everyone.

'We have got to have fair decisions. Now we have that possibility with new management in the sporting authority (Max Mosley had replaced Balestre). In the drivers' briefing today there was no theatre. It was a proper, professional job. When Max stood up to say just a few words he was sensible, intelligent and fair. I think anyone there was happy because there was no bullshit.

'I don't care (if I upset Balestre). I think for once we all must say what we feel. That's how it should be. In the past there have been (expletive) rules which say you cannot speak what you're thinking, you are not allowed to say someone made a mistake. We are in a modern world! We are racing professionals! There is a lot of money involved, a lot of image and we cannot say what we feel. We are not allowed because if you say what you feel you get banned, you get penalties, you pay money, you get disqualified, you lose your licence. Is that a fair way of working? It is not. I said what I thought (in 1989) and what took place afterwards was theatre.'

. . . *a perceived injustice 12 months old could still smoulder within the man and then become a fire*

The crash of 1990? 'If you get (expletived) every single time when you're trying to do your job cleanly and properly by the system, by other people taking advantage of it, what should you do? Stand behind and say "thank you, yes, thank you". No, you should fight for what you think is right. And I really felt that I was fighting for something that was correct because I was (expletived) in the winter and I was (expletived) when I got pole. I tell you, if pole had been on the good side last year, nothing would have happened. I would have got a better start. It was a result of a bad decision. And we all know why, and the result was the first corner. I did contribute to it yes, but it was not my responsibility.'

What you make of this is up to you, which is why I've quoted Senna at such length, repetitions and all because, like the official presentation of Senna at Didcot, it is of more than temporal interest. I have to say Senna at Suzuka astonished many listeners — that a perceived injustice 12 months old could still smoulder within the man and then become a fire; that, equally, Senna would allow fate to control the events at Turn One rather than control them himself, '*I did contribute to it, yes, but it was not my responsibility*'.

Paradoxically, perhaps, Senna would say three years later and in another context 'the downside of Formula 1 is the political side, and the decisions on the political side are not always correct or fair, but you have to accept them if you want to be in Formula 1 because you have no choice. It's a general thing in sport, not just Formula 1'.

Again, what you make of this is up to you. Who knew what fires burned eternally inside Senna, or their strength? Who knew if they had been even largely doused in 1994, when he spoke the words above? He spoke them three months after cuffing Irvine. That was in no way political but it certainly flowed from a perceived injustice in the way Irvine behaved.

Some of the child remained within the man, a self-perceived purity of purpose, a near desperate vehemence at betrayal. This vehemence is essential to the compulsions of the man, how he thinks and why he thinks like that. You are free to disagree with his reasoning and his conclusions. I only say that they exist.

I wonder if he ever sees contradictions in the reasoning. He can certainly separate the parts of himself, moving from one to another as smoothly as he can drive a racing car. Here is another part, speaking at Adelaide, the final race of 1991. It's after the first qualifying session and he has provisional pole.

Dry qualifying in Australia where, inevitably, Senna took pole.

'Because the Championship is resolved you tend to think things are going to get easier. Once you get back into the car you have to push as hard as ever. Today was good. I had no problems, but we must work at improving the balance of the car. The big problem here is the low level of grip. Although the car is quick it is not quite right for the conditions and we still have a lot of work to do.'

After the second session, and pole: 'This is very special because it was the last qualifying session of the year and it is fantastic for me to have scored the sixtieth pole position of my career. It was a target I set myself this season and we just made it at the last minute. The mechanics did a marvellous job repairing the gearbox problem I had this morning and cleaning up the extinguishant which was all over the back of the car (the gearbox caught fire). They gave me a nice handling car and this result is as much down to their efforts as to mine'.

It rained on the Sunday, rained so hard they stopped the race 14 laps into it, Senna leading. Contrast his words on safety here with his feelings on Suzuka, 1990. 'I only started it because I felt a strong obligation to the team, which has supported me so well over the years, and with the Constructors' Championship in mind. It was agreed that I would see how things developed and would be free to stop if the conditions became really impossible. I do not believe we should have started the race in these conditions but I realise the officials have a tough decision to make under these circumstances and we have obligations to spectators and sponsors.'

A further contradiction, this one only superficial. Senna had at least matured to the point where he regarded very wet races as unacceptable risks: a man far removed from the newcomer who, in a storm at Monaco in 1984, expressed his vehemence that the race had been stopped as he caught Prost for the lead.

And a last contradiction. Senna was presented with his 1991 World Championship at the annual FISA prizegiving in Paris in December 1991. He employed his charm. He presented Balestre with his helmet and said 'we have had our differences in the past, Jean-Marie. I don't want to go back to it. I know you want to have something from me as a personal thing. As far as I'm concerned, today I try to close any misunderstanding between us. What happened in the past is past'.

The burying — again.

• CHAPTER FOUR •

In Mansell's Wake

*The guy is a very intense person full stop but he was quite help-
ful, very open at times. Sometimes I'd get the feeling he was a bit
lonely, people scared to go and sit down and chat. It's like seeing
one of the top models from the catwalk. I'm sure it is a fact that
they are lonely as sin because nobody approaches them, but at
the end of the day everyone is flesh and blood. — Mark Blundell*

THE START OF every Formula 1 season is a step into the unknown,
as Frank Williams keeps insisting. While you've been working so
hard the other teams have too, and as Williams did once say, 'three
months down the road we may have made a balls of it'.

I propose to examine 1992 from two directions, the foreground and
the background. The background is worth it. In 1989 and 1990 Mark
Blundell acted as the official Williams test driver, then joining
Brabham, a struggling team, in 1991. He managed a sixth place in
Belgium and, though he didn't qualify in Canada, he manipulated
the car well enough to earn general praise. McLaren hired him as
their test driver.

'I clocked on, as you might say, in late 1991, driving the McLaren
MP4/6 at Estoril. My relationship with Ayrton had been to say hello
and we'd acknowledge each other. Obviously I'd been at circuits

This picture distills the theme of the whole book: Senna the maximiser, getting the most out of what he had whether it could win Championships or not (Proaction).

Gerhard Berger spent the winter testing and getting fit so he could out-match Senna, but when Senna put the power down Berger was in trouble. Phoenix, USA, 1991.

The moods of the man.

Above *Senna won Phoenix from Alain Prost . . .*

Left *. . . but looked pensive.*

Top right *Senna and Berger, seen here at Phoenix, remained friends and nothing shook that friendship.*

Middle right *The benign presence of the father, a frequent visitor to the Grands Prix. He has a wonderful ripple of a name: Milton Guirado Theodoro da Silva. Ayrton's actually da Silva, too, but prefers his middle name – Senna – for racing.*

Right *Monaco, 1991, and the control that gets you pole.*

Monaco, 1991, and the speed that gets you your fourth win of the season out of four.

Nigel Mansell, second at Monaco, bearhugs Senna.

Medication in Mexico, 1991, after he crashed heavily at the corner called Peralta during qualifying.

Mastery at the Hungaroring 1991, leading Riccardo Patrese and Mansell. Senna won.

The man who wanted to know everything. You cycle a circuit, looking, gauging, remembering, thinking.

The man who wanted to know everything. You stoop to conquer, looking, dissecting, probing, thinking.

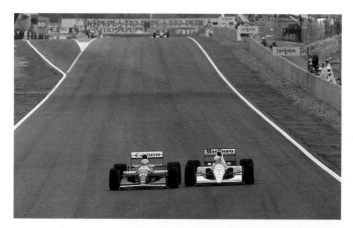

Willpower against willpower, nerve against nerve as Mansell and Senna almost touch at full bore in Spain, 1991.

The crux of the 1991 World Championship at Suzuka, Japan. Mansell tracks Senna, preparing to make his move.

Mansell felt his brakes go soft at the corner at the end of the straight.

The aftermath, Mansell running back, Senna long gone.

The last pit stop before the Championship.

The hard season, 1992, Mansell in the Williams almost impossible to catch. Here Senna concentrates in Mexico.

Main Picture
Victory at Monza in 1992 but Mansell had already taken the Championship.

Inset *One of the greatest laps ever driven. Senna, second row of the grid, is engulfed at the start of the 1993 European Grand Prix at Donington. He's masked by the Sauber of Karl Wendlinger (no 29).*

Main picture
*Moments later
he's behind the
Williams of
Hill, Prost
leading.*

Inset *Moments
later he's not
behind the
Williams of
Hill . . . or
Prost.*

In the wet–dry–wet–dry everybody was vulnerable to Senna. Here he is, predatory, stalking Hill.

The inside track, Donington, 11 April, 1993.

Main picture
*The way
Donington
should be
remembered: a
man alone
under his
heaven.*

Inset *Senna's
last pit stop.
Nothing can
stop him now.*

Senna arrived at the last minute at Imola in 1993 and had an unhappy weekend, crashing in qualifying and practice, then walking away from the race when the Marlboro McLaren's hydraulics failed.

Senna at Monaco in 1993 with his girlfriend Adriene Galisteu, a Brazilian model (John Townsend).

The beginnings of the emotional farewell to McLaren. Senna and Ron Dennis embrace after Senna won in Japan, 1993 (Proaction).

The fly-past for the photographers at Estoril, January 1994 (ICN UK Bureau).
Farewell (ICN UK Bureau).

where he'd been and I'd done the testing at Williams. If you sit in a car like the Williams you'll make your presence felt because of the machinery, and Ayrton is going to want to know who's driving it, but when I first went to McLaren all I knew of Senna was that he was the great Ayrton Senna. I'd seen him from the Brabham, coming past me many, many times.

'When he reached Formula 1 I'd only just started motor racing so he was one of the guys I followed to see how he got on. Now I was chief test driver. At that point other guys tested as well, Allan McNish, Jonathan Palmer, but anything that was going to be done I did. It was a big role because you're talking about one of the best teams over the last 10 years and lots of things will go through your hands. It's only going to get to the race driver when you've tried it. The team will put a seal of approval on it and say "yeah, let's run with that". If you are handling the bulk of it you try to make sure you steer it in the right direction.

'When the McLaren MP 4/7 came out I did about 60 per cent of the work on it and I can assure you it had problems. It wasn't right straight out of the box. We put a great deal of effort into sorting it and at the point when Ayrton tried it — and ran through the first part of the season as well — I think he appreciated I was doing a reasonable job. He was — what shall I say? — quite happy with my feedback and response. He was quite happy to take a considerable amount of my say-so and my thoughts.'

Did that responsibility intimidate you?

'No, because it is not in my nature to doubt myself. That is not being cocky. It's a way of saying I am confident in what I am doing. At the same point, people can always be wrong, sure. Nine times out of 10 you're on the right side but now and again you'll make a mistake. My train of thought was that I'm a race driver as well as a tester. How would I like the car to handle in a race? What will be best for Ayrton and Gerhard when they get to the Grands Prix? I always tried to keep that in mind. It gave me a high, gave me a push.'

Were you starting to get closer to Senna as men?

'Obviously through the year I sat down with him on a number of occasions for discussions. Going through that year, I watched what went on within McLaren and outside McLaren where Ayrton was involved, and I attended a number of Grands Prix as a member of the

A long slog across 1992 chasing Mansell and Patrese – and another crash at Peralta, Mexico, in practice. This is what the McLaren looked like afterwards.

In Mexico the transmission failed after 11 laps.

McLaren team. The guy is under intense pressure from everywhere. He might give a cold-shoulder feeling to a lot of people, he might seem arrogant and that sort of thing but at some point he has to close down. There is only so much he can give. At times he flusters, at times he might react in an unusual way but he is there to do his job, which is driving the car, and there is no-one presently doing the job better. You have to understand that these days there is a lot more to a driver's life than simply the driving. But he is still focused on the prime point: what it is that is driving a racing car as quickly as possible around a track. I respect him in the way he handles the many points in a driver's life.'

The temperament and the outbursts?

'I think of it this way. My upbringing is probably a lot different to his. My culture is a lot different so our outlooks on life will be somewhat different too. For an Englishman to turn round and do what Ayrton does would be frowned upon very heavily — and maybe the other way round, too — whereas in his country it might be taken as normal. It's like watching a game of Italian football and then watching a game in our Premier League. They are completely different games, not only because of the style of the football but because of the temperaments and the mentalities.

'The thing you do have to say about Ayrton is that the guy has presence. He'll walk in somewhere and there it is, the presence. That's become bigger and bigger as he has come up through the sport and he's achieved more and more. I think he set out to achieve that from the beginning. I am sure there are a number of people who don't like the guy but I am sure that same number of people would say "being perfectly honest, we respect him 100 per cent". He was incredibly demanding and maybe some in the team got peed off at times because of his demands, but all his demands have a reason.'

Did he ever do anything magical in the car and you thought I didn't think he could do that?

'I will be perfectly honest. No. That's my feeling because when we tested together there wasn't anything out of the ordinary. However, at a Grand Prix I'd have to say he'd turn in laps which were exceptional. You know, a guy in a Grand Prix situation is always going to be more pumped up, wound up, he'll draw on everything he has — because the Grand Prix time is it, is the goal. Ayrton will go out and do what he can to the maximum because that is his make-up.

'He is very thorough in all areas. He will make sure in his own mind that everything has been done as he wants. I learnt from him: to make sure you were comfortable with what was going on but also to put demands on people in key areas to make sure the job does get done. That's not whingeing, it is being constructive — to reach the goal. If that peed people off, at the end of it the benefit is there for everybody, and that is something he works on. People also know that Ayrton will reward whatever effort they put in by what he does with the car on the track. If you can create that within a team you've got half the job covered and he does that very well.'

In the foreground, moving into the 1992 season, certain factors in the equation were known. Although Prost, now departed Ferrari, tested the Ligier he'd take 1992 as a sabbatical. It left a familiar arrangement: Mansell and Patrese in the Canon Williams Renaults, Senna and Berger in the Marlboro McLaren Hondas. The unknown? Just to take an obvious example, there were no more special qualifying tyres.

In Brazil the electrics failed after 17 laps – and anyway Senna had been no higher than third behind Mansell and Patrese.

McLaren wouldn't debut their new car (the MP4/7A) until Brazil. In that context South Africa and Mexico did not seem to carry conclusive importance as guides to the season. The way it happened they did. At Kyalami, Berger finished the first qualifying session behind Mansell, Senna third: 'Without qualifying tyres it's impossible to really go for it on a single lap with maximum grip. With race tyres the grip level is much more limited. We are using maximum down-force and it's still not enough. On race tyres the car goes light in some of the corners, so it feels very different to drive and it's easier to spin.'

Senna moved up to second in final qualifying — 'a clear run but we are just not fast enough'. *That* would be the story of 1992. Here is the evidence:

Friday untimed		Qualifying	
Mansell	1:16.523	Mansell	1:15.576
Patrese	1:16.758	Berger	1:16.672
Berger	1:17.163	Senna	1:16.815
Senna	1:17.344	Patrese	1:17.571

(Patrese had gear-selection problems and spun.)

Saturday untimed		Qualifying	
Mansell	1:15.804	Mansell	1:15.486
Senna	1:17.211	Senna	1:16.227
Patrese	1:17.337	Berger	1:16.877
Berger	1:17.749	Patrese	1:16.989

At the green Mansell made a swift start while Patrese, who had trac-tion control, sliced between the McLarens. Senna knew 'right from the start that after such a good getaway by Riccardo it would be almost impossible to pass him. I tried to keep the pressure on but he was a little faster than me'. Mansell, unimpeded, blitzed the opening lap — 1:28.056, Patrese 1:30.494, Senna 1:31.011 — and it went on and on and on like that for the 72 laps.

A nightmare in Mexico. During first qualifying Senna reached the Esses and the uneven track bucked the McLaren. It rotated, the brakes dragging smoke from the tyres, struck the wall nearly head-on and rotated again, this time to a halt. Senna sat trapped in the cock-pit gesturing with both hands raised to his helmet for help. 'On a track like this, with no grip and so much dirt, when you hit a bump

Left *Wet–dry in Spain. Senna ran fourth early on with Jean Alesi (Ferrari) and Berger behind.*

Above *Very wet towards the end (look at the spray). Eventually Senna spun off.*

there is really nothing you can do. It was a very hard impact and the pain was unbearable. I hit both legs violently inside the chassis and thought I had broken them.

'This was the result of having to run on a track which has proved time and again to be incompatible with modern Formula 1 cars. Things might have been different with qualifying tyres from which you get reasonable grip and you can try to recover control. With race tyres on a track as dirty and bumpy as this it's impossible. Not having qualifying tyres is, I think, a grave mistake.'

He qualified sixth next day despite a limp. It was an unhappy race after the nightmare, Mansell leading from Patrese, Senna carving space down the long straight and nuzzling in front of Schumacher to be third into Turn One. He held that until lap 12. 'I had some sort of problem with the clutch or the transmission, not a problem I have had before.' Mansell won from Patrese, Schumacher third, Berger fourth. Even with 14 races stretching to the autumn Mansell had laid a hand on the Championship although that might depend on the new McLaren, ready for Brazil two weeks after Mexico.

A difficult weekend there working on and with the new cars. Senna reached third on the grid behind, inevitably, Mansell and Patrese but only after an incident at the end of second qualifying. Mansell moved past him into the tight Bico de Pao corner. Senna holding the racing line. Mansell spun into the wall. 'I don't hold Ayrton to blame at all,' Mansell said. 'I think it was a mis-communication. I thought he'd pulled over to the right to let me by. We almost touched. The nature of that short straight and the track gave me no opportunity to come back quickly enough. I got into a half-spin, simple as that.'

'During the early stages my car suffered a serious and intermittent engine cut-out'

Senna said he only saw something happened to Mansell 'when I was out of the corner already. It happened under braking when we were both going slowly. I don't know what happened with him'. A difficult race, too. 'During the early stages my car suffered a serious and intermittent engine cut-out. The effect of this was totally unpredictable and could occur four or five times on one lap and not at all on the next. At times the cut-out was so bad it felt as if I had applied the brakes. I continued with this problem, trying to cover it in the hope that it would eventually go away while at the same time raising my arm to warn the drivers behind of my problem.' The cut-out did not go away. Senna stopped on lap 17, thirteenth. Mansell won from Patrese and Schumacher.

A wet race in Spain, and Alesi made a wild or wonderful start (depending on whether you're Italian) from the fourth row, flinging the Ferrari across towards Berger and Capelli, steadied it, pointed it more or less ahead and by then Senna had moved towards mid-track. They brushed. 'Alesi drove into me but it was wheel-to-wheel contact so we got away with it . . .'

Actually Alesi jumped the start but only by a milli-second and explained that because his grid position happened to be under the pedestrian bridge and thus shielded from the drizzle his 'rear wheels started in the dry'. Hence his start. 'I must say I was surprised to see Alesi alongside me with the light still red!' Berger joked.

Crossing the line to complete lap 1 Senna had taken Berger and Brundle to be fifth. Here, revealed by the on-board camera, was the artistry and touch of Senna. He rounded a curving left-hander easily enough but on the little straight afterwards had to catch and correct the McLaren, the steering wheel jumping towards full lock before he caught it. In the next right-hand corner he had to adjust, feel, adjust, feel, and twice his hands pumped to hold the wheel steady. The deeply astonishing aspect remains that Senna rarely makes the car look twitchy.

Mansell ticked off fastest lap to keep Patrese under control. Schumacher third. Senna fourth. The drizzle still fell but again the statistics tell everything. Lap 16:

Mansell	28m 12.586s
Patrese	at 3.214s
Schumacher	at 23.122s
Senna	at 28.024

A couple of laps later the drizzle became rain and Patrese spun off. Senna's McLaren did twitch visibly here and there on the circuit, slithered, wobbled: and the rain increased. The McLaren escaped him and, side-on, skimmed over a run-off area, returned to the track. 'I was lucky but the car aquaplaned everywhere.' With three laps left he spun again and 'this time I just couldn't hold it'.

He ran third to the end at Imola behind (of course) Mansell and Patrese. 'I had some sort of cramp in my shoulders caused by the vibration of the car and the tension involved in keeping it on the road. Although the heat was not a critical factor (Imola normally in April but this year mid-May) it did not help either. The shoulder straps of the belts compress the nerves and I was being pushed against them every time the car jumped and every time I changed gear.'

Received wisdom insists that pole position — or at worst the front row — is paramount at Monaco. Senna qualified third after a spin on his first quick lap 'through driving over the limit to try and make up the time somehow. At Monaco being on the front row of the grid is half the battle. I will have to be patient'.

How important the front row? This is how it worked itself out over

Above *Yes, this has to be Italy and it is. The fans brought company, and then settled to watch the San Marino Grand Prix at Imola.*

Below *Some brought televisions and watched it on that.*

Right *They saw Senna finish third. Here he moves past Thierry Boutsen (Ligier).*

106

the preceding decade, poleman in column one, the other man on the front in column two, winner in column three:

1982	Arnoux	Patrese	Patrese
1983	Prost	Arnoux	Rosberg
1984	Prost	Mansell	Prost
1985	Senna	Mansell	Prost
1986	Prost	Mansell	Prost
1987	Mansell	Senna	Senna
1988	Senna	Prost	Prost
1989	Senna	Prost	Senna
1990	Senna	Prost	Senna
1991	Senna	Modena	Senna

The front is a huge advantage if you're Prost or Senna. Otherwise it guarantees nothing and the physical constrictions of Monaco — the armco tight onto you, the back-markers who can make you crazy — often fashion races which defy prediction. And 1992 fashioned one of those.

Mansell, pole, booted the Williams towards Ste Devote, Patrese tucking in, Senna gathering speed. He stayed on the inside and sprinted. Into Ste Devote, an eye-of-the-needle right, Patrese was outside him, slotting onto the racing line. It gave Senna the width of a car clear. Enough . . .

Senna sprinted so hard that Mansell, on the racing line, moved across him. Senna lifted, rode the kerbing and followed Mansell up the hill. Senna would stay as close as possible because he knew the facts behind the folklore. *There is always the possibility of the unexpected here.*

Mansell cranked up his pace and, Senna would say, no way could I stay with him. Nearing lap 20, Mansell led by 15 seconds. Translating that into distance, each time Mansell eased around the Station hairpin and disappeared through the righthander after it, Senna had not yet come into sight on the descent to the hairpin. By lap 60, Mansell stroking the Williams home, the lap had become 30 seconds. Ten laps later nothing had changed. Then everything changed. 'Coming through the tunnel,' Mansell said, 'I almost lost it and the back end went down. I felt immediately that I had a puncture. The problem was that I was halfway from the pits and I had to drive slowly to get to them. I estimate I lost between 10 and 15 seconds doing that. I had a longer pit stop than normal and as I came out I saw Ayrton go by.'

Mansell set off furiously, wheelspin, dust flying, the lot, and prepared to give a performance. Mansell cut past a back marker and another. That was lap 73 of 78. Senna 5.159 seconds distant.

	Senna	Mansell
Lap 74	1:24.007	1:21.598
Lap 75	1:25.108	1:23.388

The lap 74 stood as the fastest of the race. That lap 75 brought Mansell to within 1.960 seconds. 'For the last five or six laps I had nothing left to give,' Senna said. 'My tyres were finished and I had no grip. I knew Nigel would catch me on fresh tyres. I gave it everything.'

They came upon J.J. Lehto (Dallara). Into the chicane after the tunnel Lehto had Senna behind and it allowed Mansell to nose up. On the harbour front Lehto clung to the right, opening a path for Senna and keeping it open for Mansell. Senna remained calm, did not sacrifice his calmness to the moment. He remained on the racing line. Mansell lurking, darting, thrusting left and right, probing.

	Senna	*Mansell*
Lap 76	1:26.776	1:26.848
Lap 77	1:28.114	1:28.132

Last lap: Senna resolute on the racing line, follow-my-leader through the eye-of-the-needle, follow-my-leader up the hill, Senna inside for the curve into Casino, Mansell slightly wider; tight together through Casino, follow-my-leader on the bump-bore-bump to Mirabeau — a potential passing place but Mansell fractionally too far away — tight round the Station Hairpin, Mansell braking so hard he drew smoke from the left front tyre; accelerating from the crown of Mirabeau so ferociously the Williams bucked.

The race turned on the chicane after the tunnel. If Mansell could find enough momentum into, through and out of the tunnel he might thrust past at the chicane. They entered the tunnel nose-to-tail and Senna maintained that on the flight to the chicane. Senna wrestled the McLaren through it. Along the harbour front Mansell swarmed, making a last inside-outside lunge into the twist of Rascasse, the left-

Senna won Monaco but only because Mansell, fearing a puncture, stopped late for tyres.

right-right before the finishing straight. Senna nursed the racing line and Mansell went wide, wide, wide to go round him. Not possible within the confines of Monaco.

Senna won by 0.215 seconds. 'I knew he would try everything,' Senna said. 'I knew we would be in for a major war in the last three laps. It was exciting but very difficult because he was several seconds faster than me and I had no grip to put the power down. It was like on ice. Fortunately I only had three or four laps that way. On the straights it was like a drag race, wheelspin in third and fourth gears.'

Mansell didn't complain about Senna's blocking. 'Ayrton was perfectly entitled to do what he did.'

Senna took pole in Canada, his first since Australia 1991, and made a semi-joke. 'It's been such a long time I can hardly remember.' Senna now had a record 61 poles. (Jim Clark was next with 33.) The Canadian Grand Prix became a potential detonation from the moment Senna outgunned Mansell at the start. Mansell had a look or two, laid pressure. Senna sacrificed nothing to the pressure, circling evenly, precisely. Patrese tracked Mansell, Berger tracked Patrese.

'In the opening stages it was impossible to overtake so it was a question of just waiting a little bit,' Berger said. 'The first six cars were together but there was too much risk involved in trying to overtake and I decided to stay behind Patrese. Everyone knows that if you want to try really hard to overtake you have to go off line where the track is dirty and you lose grip.' Berger proved this by having a joust at Patrese at the chicane before the start-finish straight, backed off and murmured *never going to work.*

Senna controlled the queue, no matter that he ran at a pace slower than the Williamses would achieve if they could get by. Travelling to the chicane on lap 14 Mansell made his move. The chicane is a right-flick, left-flick. Mansell moved off the racing line — Berger, wide behind Patrese, enjoying an unobstructed view, murmured *never going to work.* Mansell locked brakes and slewed across Senna, slewed across the chicane, slewed across Senna again onto the start finish straight. The wounded Williams described an arc and halted facing the oncoming traffic.

An ordinary Formula 1 furore. 'He realised he couldn't brake in time,' Senna said, 'so he lined the car up with the middle of the kerb and hoped to clear it but he hit it with such force that he appeared to land on the car's nose.' Mansell made savage noises and tried to protest, but was turned away. Senna led to lap 37 when the electrics failed.

At Magny-Cours Senna made, by his own confession, a bad start. Berger nipped past and Senna muscled him, two wheels off, didn't get through. Schumacher attacked Senna.

Approaching the Adelaide hairpin, Schumacher inserted the Benetton to the inside and they thumped, Schumacher ramming the rear of the McLaren and battering it. 'Gerhard and I ended up side by side at the first corner,' Senna said. 'That was close but OK. I followed him down the straight, he braked very late so I was being careful, and then Schumacher came up and hit me from behind. I think he totally misjudged his speed and his braking point for that corner — considering that it was the first lap — and he could not stop.'

> ### 'The ice-cool bit is part of his make-up. He is totally single-minded, selfish even'

The Championship had virtually gone. Senna stood by the side of the track, helmet clasped in both hands behind his back, watching the race. He looked sanguine. Mansell won: Mansell 66 points, Patrese 34, Schumacher 26, Senna 18.

Mansell bestrode all aspects of Silverstone, particularly the race. Senna, fourth, duelled with Brundle, third, stirred undercurrents from memory of their duelling in Formula 3. Senna described it as 'a good clean fight. I was pushing like hell the whole race and I was surprised I could keep up such a performance under such pressure for so long. On some corners I could catch him, on some he was going away. I tried many times. Sometimes the backmarkers helped, sometimes they didn't'. Eventually the transmission failed.

Brundle discusses the undercurrents. 'Ayrton does tend to think the whole world is against him. He's strange, really. One day he'll talk to you, another day he won't. He never gets involved in small talk. For instance. we've never got together and chatted about the old days in Formula 3. That's not the way he is. He keeps his distance. The ice-cool bit is part of his make-up. He is totally single-minded, selfish even. That partly explains his success. It must be difficult having the constant pressure. He is, let's face it, one of the world's best known people.'

Mansell beat Patrese by 39.094 seconds and stirred a fervour of such intensity that sections of the crowd came on the track before the race finished.

At Hockenheim Senna qualified third and intended to run the race on a single set of tyres to counter the advantage the Williams held. Mansell pitted on lap 14, giving Patrese the lead, Senna second, Mansell emerging third. He caught Senna comfortably enough. Boring down on the first chicane Mansell placed the Williams out to the outside and they ran abreast, the chicane flooding towards them. Senna outbraked him and they waltzed through juddering the kerbs.

Mansell crowded Senna, had a nibble to one side — Senna covering that — and at the second chicane Mansell plunged, bisecting the chicane. He recovered, re-caught Senna and flicked by. Patrese pitted, needed 13 laps to overhaul Schumacher and set off after Senna, who he could see.

'I didn't know if I could cope with Riccardo. He had more top speed and his tyres were in better condition. The last 10 laps were very worrying because I had bad vibrations from the tyres, but the only way to get onto the podium was to take a chance and go through without stopping.' Patrese caught Senna but, into the Ostkurve, Patrese locked all four wheels. Senna stole off. Patrese clamped onto him again and, two laps left, loomed like a predator. Those two laps demand exploration because Patrese had more power, fresher tyres and (in theory) around Hockenheim there's no hiding place.

Beginning the second last lap Patrese weaved a little, half-searching for an opening. Senna constructed a small gap round the graceful right-hander after the start-finish straight but would be vulnerable on the long slog to the first chicane, a juicy environment for grabbing a 'tow' and frisking by. The slog unfolds rightwards and Senna selected the inside, moving to mid-track for the chicane. Patrese had to follow.

Another straight. Senna to mid-track, Patrese pressing up; a left-hander, Senna far to the right. Patrese grasping the gap inside. He'd done it. Senna didn't back off and held on outside, finger-tip touch, balance, desire. Patrese hadn't done it. Patrese had to follow. Senna's

Senna took pole in Canada but the electrics failed half way through the race.

impetus carried the McLaren into the opposite kerbing and the car hopped. On the rush to the complex, Patrese searching, Senna held midtrack. Patrese had to follow. They came through the complex and Senna had set his fastest time of the race, one minute 42.272. To produce it at such a moment, on tyres some 186 miles old, is eloquent enough.

They began the final lap. To the first chicane Senna squeezed out a little 'lead' and that robbed Patrese of any chance. Patrese had to follow. Through the chicane Patrese squeezed, so that exiting it, he was closer, getting to within striking distance. To the second chicane Patrese feinted inside and Senna feinted to block. Patrese took a sling-shot outside and Senna flicked to block. His rear wheels nearly stroked the front wheels of Patrese. Patrese flicked to the inside again but Senna had *already* blocked that. Patrese had to follow.

The rush to the complex: Senna to the right but angling left, left, left onto the racing line to enter the complex. Patrese moved inside and they ran level. Senna flicked further left, braked impossibly late — finger-tip touch, balance, desire and sat on the racing line. The braking pitched him in front of Patrese. Patrese braked hard, smoke coming from the rear wheels, and it cast him onto the grass, spinning and spinning. Patrese drew a shroud of dust. 'I tried to attack Senna on the last corner,' he said, 'and go through a hole but he closed the door and I braked on the dirt. I went off and did a 360 degree and it was impossible to get back on the track. Senna was not unfair, he defended his position. A long, hard and fair fight.'

Mansell could secure the Championship in Hungary but the background to that weekend became a strange mess of a thing into which Ayrton Senna moved with seismic effect.

To recap. In 1990 Mansell retired from Ferrari and Formula 1 but Williams absolutely needed a front runner and gave Mansell everything he demanded not to retire but to join them instead. Approaching the Hungaroring, 1992, Mansell had delivered everything except the Championship and stood poised to deliver that now. He entered negotiations with Williams for 1993 believing himself in a very strong position.

He wasn't.

Williams were long rumoured to have a contract with Prost for 1993, something which would scarcely displease Renault and Elf. However Prost wouldn't (surely) be prepared to accept what Patrese accepted: Mansell having undisputed Number One status and constant use of the spare car. Would Mansell accept that Prost couldn't agree to this?

Prost (we assumed) would stipulate a clause in any contract insisting his partner wasn't Senna. Mansell (we assumed) wouldn't want Senna. Frank Williams found himself in a very strong position. The three drivers who might win the World Championship in 1993 wanted his team badly. Senna had an offer from Ferrari (reportedly 23 million dollars) but, Ferrari in more than usual disarray, would have to spend the following year developing their car. With unusual candour, a Ferrari spokesman said: 'Senna is our number one target but we have told him we do not think we can win the Championship in 1993 and we must work for 1994. If we do not get Senna we will have Gerhard Berger. That is the most probable thing'.

Certainly Senna's future at McLaren would be influenced by the rumoured withdrawal of Honda from Formula 1. What engine could McLaren have and would it stand a chance against Renault?

Mansell pondered the permutations. Prost pondered them and Senna pondered them.

A bad start in France, both Williams already gone. Nor would Senna complete a lap – Michael Schumacher (Benetton) crashed into him.

While Mansell and Williams settled to the serious negotiations Senna watched and calculated. Before the race he made his move. He sought out James Hunt and imparted the information that he would be prepared to drive for Williams in 1993 *free*.

If, like Hunt, you are a commentator about to handle a race where a Briton can become your successor (Hunt the last British World Champion, 1976) and a great driver seeks you out and gives you a world exclusive with a direct bearing on the Briton about to become World Champion, you'll use it. Why select Hunt? Shrewd. The lingua franca of Formula 1 is English and most of the teams are English — particularly Williams — and most of the journalists are English, too. If you desire maximum impact this is the medium you use. As the cars formed up for the Hungarian Grand Prix, only Hunt knew. Grid:

Patrese

Mansell

Senna

Schumacher

Berger

Brundle

No hiding from Renault power at Hockenheim. Mansell won and led the Championship 86–40 from Patrese, Schumacher 33, Senna 24.

A monumental start, every driver knowing the importance of the compression into Turn One because — like Monaco — if you get there first you command the race. Mansell seemed to have made the better start and urged his car parallel with Patrese, Senna lurking, Schumacher not yet up with him. Patrese kept the power on, on, on and drew ahead, Senna clear of Schumacher. In the sweep towards Turn One the compression compressed. Patrese squeezed Mansell, forcing him to the rim and that left the outside unoccupied. Senna, braking late, slung the McLaren around Mansell, Berger eager, audacious — slinging through behind Senna.

Mansell, fourth.

The Championship moved into abeyance.

Patrese, a clear track spread before him, built a lead. Lap after lap Mansell tried to take Senna into Turn One. Lap after lap Senna stretched enough down the straight to prevent that. Senna completely ignored Patrese and protected his position. His thinking: *I am driving as well as I have ever done in my career and this sort of performance is the product of a lot of experience.*

On the BBC, the deep and sonorous voice of James Hunt delivered

116

The Hockenheim podium, Mansell within sight of the Championship.

the seismic upheaval. 'As is the nature of Grand Prix racing at this time of the year, there tends to be as much excitement in the paddock as anywhere else and, of course, the big problem for this year is the situation of three-into-two-won't-go. The Williams team have the world's three top drivers, Ayrton Senna, Alain Prost and Nigel Mansell, all trying to fit into two cars and the situation is that Alain Prost, as far as we can work out, has signed for Williams or is certainly very much committed to the Williams team for next year.

'Nigel Mansell is reported to be demanding 23 million dollars to drive for the Williams team next year which one feels . . . well certainly the Williams team are very upset about it. They feel it's much too much money for them when everyone else is queuing up. Ayrton Senna has today countered that offer and said to me that he will drive for the Williams team for nothing. He wants that to be known. He wants to win the World Championship. He wants no retainer. He said *I will drive for the Williams team for 23 million dollars less than Nigel Mansell or whatever he wants. Whatever the case is I am prepared to drive for Williams for nothing.*

'He points also to when McLaren had himself and Alain Prost in 1988. What a good season's racing it was and the problem in the team is a tremendous mess for Frank Williams to sort out. It's unenviable for him. To add to the confusion, Mansell seems to be pricing himself out of the market and is also making demands for favouritism in the team that the team are not prepared to meet.

'The problem for Senna and for Frank Williams is that not only is Nigel Mansell making demands for position and for money but Alain Prost is using everything he can — possibly with a contract, one might speculate — to block any arrival of Ayrton Senna in the team. Prost's public statements suggest he's happy to drive with Ayrton Senna but behind the scenes he's doing everything he can to make sure that Senna doesn't join the French-engined team. And this is a problem that is making Senna a very unhappy man. He says he just wants to race with anybody. He's happy to do that and I certainly agree with him.'

The story of the Hungarian Grand Prix is well-enough known: Patrese went out on lap 39 — 'I spun. I think there was some dirt on the track. The engine started to go after 20 laps and I had the feeling then that I wouldn't finish the race'. Mansell followed Senna. Berger took Mansell and Mansell re-took him. With the Championship beckoning, Mansell thought he had a puncture, pitted, came out sixth, thundered to second again.

Senna enjoyed a sufficient lead to stop for tyres himself and cruise it. His thinking: *I did not expect to win and I knew that. To have a chance I'd have had to lead from the start. As it was I made up one place (Mansell) going into the first corner and tried to stay with Riccardo for a single lap. Then I realised there was no way and I concentrated on running the race within my own limitations. Riccardo dropped out and I pressed harder but towards the end I had to stop for tyres. The vibration was so bad that I could hardly see the track and I worried that an electrical component might be damaged.*

After the race Senna spoke to Frank Williams, who hadn't of course heard Hunt on the BBC, and then went public himself. 'My only motivation is to win. I do not want to race if I cannot win or at least be very competitive. I think next year Williams is going to be the best team and I want a car with the possibility to win every race. Money is secondary to me because, thank God, I'm in a very good financial position. The money is not relevant. The reason I have told Frank I am available for free is to show my motivation. Unfortunately

Hungary, and unbelievably Senna would be second an instant or two after
this photograph was taken.

Gallant gesture. Senna won the Hungarian Grand Prix but couldn't stop
Mansell taking the Championship.

there are some people who don't want me to go to Williams, for reasons which have nothing to do with the sport. I don't agree with that because I know we would have a fantastic year in 1993 if I went there.

'I cannot understand a multi-national company (Renault), which spends millions of dollars a year in Formula 1, and takes decisions based on the nationality of the drivers, and not on their competence and motivation. This is a World Championship and it should not favour drivers of certain nationalities. But because I am Brazilian I am an inferior person. What should count is the seriousness, competence and worth of the driver, not the place where he was born. That is why I told Frank I was ready to drive for free.'

'. . . *because Senna would drive for nothing, I, the new World Champion, had to accept a massive reduction in remuneration . . .*'

Mansell recounts how, three days after Hungary, 'I was telephoned by a Williams director who said he had been instructed to tell me that, because Senna would drive for nothing, I, the new World Champion, had to accept a massive reduction in remuneration from the figure agreed in Hungary, considerably less than I am receiving this year. If I did not, Senna was ready to sign "that night". I rejected this offer and said if these were the terms Williams had better go ahead and sign Senna'.

The rumour hardened that Williams had Prost, as did the rumour that it blocked any move for Senna, who said 'Prost has a contract and a clause in there which vetoes me driving and there is nothing you can do about it'. Rumours floated that Mansell would go to IndyCar racing with the Paul Newman-Carl Haas team.

At Spa, Senna finished fifth. In the record books it will always appear thus, Schumacher winning from Mansell, Patrese and Brundle. Before the race Senna revealed his thinking: *If you have the possibility to work on a car and engine to make it competitive you can stand that. When you don't feel the possibility exists it's pointless.*

A little rain fell but no driver chose wet tyres. Senna, front row, took the La Source hairpin from Mansell, pole. That couldn't be sustained through Spa's fast reaches. Truly, there was no hiding place here. Mansell clambered. By lap 2 the rain intensified — no spray from wheels yet — and Mansell went by. At the 'Bus Stop' left-right, Patrese went by also, Senna granting him a wide berth.

Next lap Mansell pitted for wets, and Alesi, and Gugelmin (Jordan), Mansell rejoined fourteenth. Mist gathered in the trees round the circuit, thick folds of it, clinging and cloying. On lap 4 Schumacher pitted, and Boutsen (Ligier), and Gachot (Venturi) and Suzuki (Footwork). On lap 5 Brundle pitted, and Hakkinen, and Gabriele Tarquini (Fondmetal), and Karl Wendlinger (March), and Stefano Modena (Jordan), and Ukyo Katayama (Venturi), and Lehto. On lap 6 Patrese pitted, and Ivan Capelli (Ferrari), and de Cesaris, and Eric Van de Poele (Fondmetal). Next lap in came Johnny Herbert (Lotus), and Emanuele Naspetti (March). By pitting, Patrese gave the lead to Senna but the drivers' virtual unanimity on tactics was clear.

At lap 8, the tyre stops completed, 23 cars were out on the circuit, 21 employing wets. Gianni Morbidelli (Minardi) did not. Ayrton Senna did not. His thinking: *Staying out represented my only chance. The car was at the edge of controllability but I judged I had nothing to lose. If the drizzle stopped I would have been in good shape.*

This extraordinary man balanced his skill against a circuit of great speed and danger stretching 4.333 miles (6.974km), a decision compounded of its own danger. At Spa drizzle may become a storm at any moment; the storm may be isolated to one part of the 4.333 miles, drizzle elsewhere, drying in other parts. The drizzle increased.

	Senna	Patrese	Mansell
Lap 8	2:19.910	2:16.690	2:19.003
Lap 9	2:19.466	2:18.116	2:16.817
Lap 10	2:20.337	2:17.648	2:17.240
Lap 11	2:23.878	2:18.084	2:18.357
Lap 12	2:23.778	2:21.442	2:17.360
Lap 13	2:25.923	2:16.145	2:17.937
Lap 14	2:30.780	2:16.750	2:16.464

On lap 8 Senna led Patrese and Mansell by 12 seconds. You can see how fast both were catching him. Picture it: the descent to Eau Rouge and a film of water on the circuit, spray in cascades and plumes and fountains, Senna keeping the McLaren on a tight rein, the car never *oscillating*. You couldn't tell his adhesion came from dry tyres, Patrese and Schumacher and Brundle eager on wets. Someone once spoke of the 'unearthly' skills of Jim Clark. The comparison with the descent to Eau Rouge on 30 August 1992 is direct and valid.

Out in the country Patrese lunged, the spray from Senna coating Patrese's visor in a shower of droplets and Senna closed the door at well over 100mph. Patrese had him at the Bus Stop, Senna deciding not to contest it. Schumacher tried at a righthander, spray on his visor now, and Senna closed the door again.

A gesture only. Schumacher went by — Senna contesting it briefly, almost as if decorum demanded that — and Brundle too, making Senna sixth. He had to come in, and did, but the wind which might have borne the drizzle away with it dropped. If the wind had risen at dripping, infuriating Spa and the track begun to dry Senna would have stayed out, content for the others to go faster and faster than he could. During the drying they'd need second tyre stops — for

The podium, the Hungaroring – Mansell, Senna, Berger – and every face tells a story.

dries — and he'd be in the lead once more. The imperative which held Senna: *I hung on but the drizzle never did stop and the choice was taken from me.* His stop, on lap 15, made him thirteenth. Immediately he moved towards the pace.

	Senna	*Mansell*
Lap 16	2:20.530	2:15.017
Lap 17	2:18.319	2:13.250
Lap 18	2:16.860	2:14.297

By lap 27 Senna lay seventh, reading the weather, feeling the surface of the track. The drizzle eased creating a dry line. He came in for dries and that cost him only one place. His thinking: *I picked a safe time to stop for tyres and I'd just learnt that the mechanics get a bonus for every point. I decided to go for it and give them two points instead of one.*

Although the race was far beyond him he covered the 4.333 miles in under two minutes. Devilish, shifting Spa, some parts dryer than other parts. Senna spun full round, set off again, slicks glistening. He set fastest lap — subsequently bettered by Schumacher — and on lap 43 out of 44 took Hakkinen for fifth place. The mechanics had their bonus. Down towards Eau Rouge he slip-streamed Hakkinen, might have taken him on the descent, wasn't close enough. They breasted the hill and guess who had the dry line? Schumacher won, beating Mansell by 36.595 seconds, Senna one minute 8.369 seconds behind Schumacher.

The record books, those books which give the results of the races in statistics, will — and do — have Senna for ever in an ordinary fifth place an age from Schumacher and Mansell. Sometimes it goes like that.

Clark estimated he drove his greatest race at the Nurburgring in a storm in 1962. The start went wrong and on the first lap he may well have overtaken 13 cars. He was — and is — held for ever by the statistics in an ordinary fourth place 42.1 seconds behind the winner, Graham Hill. Jackie Stewart, a sometime critic of Senna, can't finitely decide his own greatest race and selects two: the Nurburgring in a storm in 1968 when he beat Hill by more than four minutes, and Monza in 1973 when an early puncture cost him a minute and put him twentieth. Monza, as Stewart explains, is a circuit where it's difficult to regain time and that is why his drive there still gives him such

Give us a push, lads. Senna spins in practice, Spa.

Thanks.

satisfaction. He was — and is — held for ever by the statistics in an ordinary fourth place 33.20 seconds behind the winner, Ronnie Peterson.

In every race you need every context. You have to try and dissect the mosaic of movement. Within half a year Senna would draw from himself a greater race than Spa 1992 — in the wet at Donington . . .

Mansell retired from Grands Prix racing at the Italian Grand Prix, Monza of course, amidst mayhem, chaos and bitterness. The race might be easy to forget under the weight of that — a Williams employee trying to dissuade Mansell while he made his speech. For the first time of which I'm aware, a World Champion announced his departure with as many as four races to run.

Senna qualified on the front row, Mansell pole. The start might have settled it: Mansell leading, Alesi — cheeky — nipping in front of Senna who outbraked him at the chicane, smoking tyres, the lot. Patrese, fourth, clearly wouldn't be fourth for long and took Alesi on the start-finish straight moving into lap 2. He set about Senna.

Senna's thinking: *After the start I didn't judge I could maintain my position but Nigel only pulled away a relatively small amount and I was able to stay in touch. Then Riccardo caught me quite easily and made a very good overtaking manoeuvre. He went on the brakes really late and I thought he was going to go straight into the sandtrap.*

That happened at the first chicane, Patrese locking wheels but making it. In time Mansell allowed Patrese into the lead but Patrese spun. Mansell went out with hydraulic failure and Senna won. His thinking: *I was always able to close the gap in traffic so I kept going at my own pace, sustaining the pressure in the hope they might crack. The performance was the best I could get out of the technical situation.*

End of the season, the Championship gone, Mansell going, Prost (surely) coming and three races to run. Senna finished third in Portugal on a damp but drying track. 'The conditions were abnormal and therefore the wear and performance of the tyres also abnormal. On my second set I started to think we would need a third one. I was doing my best in second place when the team called me in for a precautionary change. On my third set the car felt really strange, almost as though it was running on three wheels. I'd never experienced that before. It was the same when I changed onto the fourth set, then it improved and finally went completely mad over the last few laps. At the finish they found I had a deflated tyre.' Abnormal? Evidently a front wing endplate hadn't been right.

After Portugal Senna went seismic again.

There is mounting speculation that McLaren might get Renault engines. Would that help you change your mind about staying with McLaren next year?

'Well, I wouldn't be able to give you a short answer because everything is far too complicated. The one thing I will say is that this is supposed to be a World Drivers' Championship. We had two fantastic Championships — sports Championships last year and this year. We had, in my opinion, two very bad ones in 1989 and 1990, and they were a consequence of unbelievable politics going on and bad behaviour by some people. I think we are coming back to the same situation. It's impossible to accept somebody coming to a team — in the February of the year, a signed contract, a veto (jerks thumb) for myself and himself too (jerks thumb towards Mansell next to him) and eventually they change his side (Mansell's) but the veto stays for me. If Prost wants to be called the sole Champion, the three-times Champion, come back in a sportive way, maybe win another Championship.

'He should be sportive. The way he's doing it he's behaving like a coward. If he wants to be sportive, he must be prepared to race anybody in any conditions on equal terms and not the way he wants, to win the Championship. Everything has been laid out for him before you start (weary smile, gesticulating). It's like if you go into a 100 metre sprint (Mansell murmuring yes) and you want to have running shoes and everybody else should have lead shoes. That's the way he wants to race. This is not racing (gesticulating animatedly). This is bad to all of us. That's it.' Berger smiles broadly, Mansell claps Senna on the back and opens his hands in agreement.

In Japan Senna retired early, parking the car 'to avoid destroying the engine'. In Australia he and Mansell crashed on lap 19. They'd jousted, Senna tracking, and here it was, another ordinary Formula 1 furore. Senna claimed that Mansell 'knew I was very close. I was closing on the limit and I could not stop my car when he braked early. There was a clear track ahead'. Mansell said 'all I know is that someone hit me up the back when I was turning in to the corner. It seems that certain people in Formula 1 can get away with anything, and

The picture of frustration. Berger is out of the Belgian Grand Prix immediately – transmission. Here Senna comes past his team-mate, Mansell and Patrese pressuring him.

A little water in the desert. Mansell broke down at Monza and Senna made no mistake.

Main picture *No joy in Adelaide. He and Mansell crashed.*

Inset *No joy in Japan. The engine let go after two laps.*

that's just been demonstrated. I'm glad to be out of it, glad to be rid of it. I didn't go near him afterwards because if I had there would have been a big fight and I don't think that's the right way to leave Formula 1. Instead I thought I would do it the honourable way, go and talk to the stewards and to my team — who didn't give me any support'.

Prost for McLaren. Mansell for the 'comfort zone' of Newman/Hass, Senna for a year off? Something like that. How could we know Senna would forego the lure of the beach, forego the alternative speed of jet ski-ing and 12 uninterrupted months in his beloved Brazil and forge himself onto Formula 1 like a smithy moulding molten metal with hammer-blows? The record books with their statistics show only part of that, but then they would, wouldn't they?

CHAPTER FIVE

The Waiting Game

I said to him 'this year you've shone even more by having a car with a lot less horsepower and a chassis which wasn't as good as the Williams'. His driving made up for it. To me that was the most important thing. Maybe he wasn't going to win the World Championship but what he did in 1993 will stay in the history of motor racing for ever. I said 'in time everybody will appreciate so much more what you have done'. — *Jo Ramirez*

IN DECEMBER 1992 Ayrton Senna flew to the Firebird Raceway in Phoenix and tested Roger Penske's IndyCar, something arranged by Emerson Fittipaldi. The car came from Senna's memory, simple by Formula 1 standards — manual gearbox, ordinary brakes rather than carbon fibre, a growling turbo.

He covered 25 laps and pushed the car to within 0.4 of Fittipaldi's time, 48.8 seconds. 'It reminded me of the old days,' Senna would say: man manipulating machine, not machine manipulating man. 'It's a funny feeling after so many years of Formula 1 to have this kind of emotion. It is suddenly like you are much younger than you really are.' Mansell, having a first run in the Newman-Hass car, did 44.9. Someone asked him about Senna coming to Indy, or at least the Indianapolis 500, and he murmured that Senna had been 'winding people up for years' and we'd see what we'd see.

Senna murmured that he kept an 'open mind' about the future and intended to return home and contemplate the options. At this stage McLaren had not announced their engine plans for 1993 and their options seemed limited. A couple of weeks later, Penske announced that Fittipaldi and young Canadian Paul Tracy would be their drivers, no third car for Senna.

'I made the right start and when I began to pull away I felt we could have done something amazing'

He said he'd test the new McLaren at Silverstone — it had a Ford HB V8 engine — and see what he'd see. He added that McLaren were asking him to sign a contract for the whole season and he wasn't about to do that. He did drive at Silverstone and set a faster time than anyone had achieved there over winter testing, faster even than Damon Hill in the Williams Renault. In principle, he said, he wanted to do all 16 Grands Prix. He signed to do the first, South Africa on 14 March, and he'd negotiate again after that. He'd partner the American Michael Andretti, Hill would partner Prost who had, of course, joined Williams.

In the opening qualifying session Senna was second fastest behind Prost. 'It was a good day without too many problems with the car and the systems,' Senna said. 'In the second part of the session it became a little slippery as too many drivers tried too hard, but other than that I am delighted with how much the team has achieved in so little time.' He held his place in second qualifying and made a beautiful start to the race, smoothing the power. Threading through the first corners he led from Hill, Prost third. Hill spun and Prost had to swerve to miss him, allowing Schumacher through. Within the initial instants of the season a great deal had already happened. Senna said 'I made the right start and when I began to pull away I felt we could have done something amazing'.

Senna carved out a lead of more than a second and a half on the first lap, Schumacher going hard, Prost falling away a little. Many would misunderstand Prost over the season, questioning his level of desire. They did not understand that he read a whole season, not just its initial instants; nor understand that he read a whole race, too, and saw the South African Grand Prix as 72 laps, not just the next corner. He settled, set fastest lap and slipped neatly past Schumacher into a right-hander, quickly, quickly closed on Senna.

He attacked, Senna defended. On the start-finish straight Prost feinted, carved across the other way, seemed to have won the inside, Senna defended that. Next lap Prost did have the inside but Senna kept his foot down, kept the lead. In a sense Senna could only buy time. The Williams and its Renault engine were too strong. On lap 23 Prost snuggled up along the start-finish straight and moved out earlier giving him a crucial few metres more to put the car where he wanted to put it. Schumacher plundered a gap, Senna third. 'The car was good at first but then at one corner it became undriveable. I thought I might have had a puncture but I realised it was an electrical problem of some sort. Prost and Schumacher were on me immediately. I radioed asking for different pressures on the new tyres when I came in just to try and help me a little bit but unfortunately the car was very bad.' Senna and Schumacher pitted the lap after Prost took the lead. Senna was back out faster to reclaim second place.

It's 1993 and now Prost has the Williams. Senna led South Africa, but not for long. Prost (2) takes Schumacher and soon will take Senna.

Senna had Schumacher, forceful, directly behind and on lap 40 Schumacher tried it on the inside of a right-hander, Senna following the racing line. They touched. The McLaren pitched but Senna caught it. Schumacher — out. Rain fell in the later stages and as that broadened into a genuine thunderstorm Senna followed Prost home at an almost artistically slow speed. To make a Formula 1 car go fast is what they do. To harness it as if on sheet-ice is another artform altogether.

Before that? How you drive the undriveable for some 100 plus miles, the final few laps through standing water, and make it look smooth and natural can only be explained by an awesome hypersensitivity which corrects and re-corrects constantly: and this at speeds the ordinary motorist never reaches once in his life.

Blundell came third. 'It was great to be on the podium with two of the greatest drivers of the decade. Ayrton felt something for me because he knew what I'd gone through the year before, testing but not racing. Now I was up there on the podium with him. He put his arm round me and said "well done" and that was like a thank you for the work I'd done. But there's another side to things.

'The year before, testing at Monza, for 85 per cent of the day I lapped quicker than he did. Eventually we both got into the same time areas but he was standing studying the telemetry to see where I had been quicker. It got to the end of the day. I was due to go back to the UK. The only person available to take me to the airport was Joseph, the masseur-trainer guy. Joseph had to ask Ayrton if it was OK to leave. I was there in the motorhome. Ayrton said "no, you stay here". He didn't need Joseph, he would be in a de-brief for another hour, another hour and a half — it was a bit of psychology if you like. *Mark, you've caused me some aggravation today. You find your own way home.* As soon as he refused Joseph I said "OK, I'll make my own way to the airport" because I knew that was the way Ayrton was working . . .'

Senna qualified on the second row in Brazil and Prost led immediately. Senna moved inside Hill. The leadership elongated: Prost-gap-Senna-gap-Hill, Prost setting fastest lap, Senna seeming to shed Hill. On Hill lay all manner of pressure: the mythology of his father Graham; the fact that after only two races with Brabham he'd got himself the most coveted Formula 1 seat and in South Africa promptly spun so early — inexperience — and then crashed, no fault of his own, but increasing the pressure.

Around Interlagos Hill bedded himself in. He didn't let Schumacher hustle him into error and towards lap 10 felt confident enough to draw up to Senna and prepare an assault. 'I was not intimidated by the fact that here is Senna and I'm going to try and overtake him,' Hill says. Through the left-hander to the start-finish straight Hill drew up and up. Down the broad, undulating start-finish straight Senna tried to mask the middle ready for a swoop into Turn One, a left. Hill pulled out from his slipstream to mid-track.

They travelled towards Turn One virtually together. Would Senna turn in before him? Could Hill keep his nerve and take and hold the inside as Senna came across? Yes. 'Fantastic. I loved it. No, you don't let yourself become emotional . . .'

Hill accelerated, just as the drizzle began, and Schumacher moved on Senna. Would Schumacher press Senna back to fourth? An irrelevant question. Senna peeled off into the pits on lap 24 but kept on past McLaren to the stop-go penalty bay where he sat motionless for 10 seconds.

The moment Mark Blundell (Ligier) treasures. Senna offers sincere congratulations.

'I couldn't believe it. It seems I was penalised because I overtook someone under a yellow flag — I think it was Comas — but the guy lifted off to let me through! The people who make these decisions should have a different way of implementing them because it was a big mistake. I was very angry. I'd only been lapping the car which had let me past.'

(An insight from Ramirez, McLaren's team co-ordinator: 'Ayrton is calm in the car but he can get excited because it's an excitable sport. Sometimes when there is a mistake, or a misunderstanding, he can come up on the radio very excited and swearing. Yet somehow his emotions and his excitement don't seem to interfere with his driving. It's as if one part of his brain is driving the car very calmly and another part is shouting *what's going on?* He can be volatile and hard with everyone else but his driving never alters. Maybe it's even better'.)

Senna resumed fourth. The drizzle continued and he came in for wet tyres a lap before Hill. Prost stayed out — a misunderstanding (!) over the radio because he thought the pits weren't ready — and it cost him the race. Christian Fittipaldi crashed and Prost ran over the debris, slithered into the gravel trap. The pace car circled, the cars bunched behind it in the order they reached it: Hill, inheriting Prost's lead, then a backmarker — Derek Warwick (Footwork) — then Senna. The rain passed and on lap 38 the pace car melted into the pits. Senna dealt with Warwick and reached towards Hill. The hunt was on.

Senna read the drying track and pitted for dries: 7.21 seconds stationary. Hill stayed out a further lap and pitted: 6.41 seconds stationary. As a backdrop, the crowd made an immense noise, whistling and cheering. Would Senna go by in the lead before Hill emerged? Senna rounded the left-hander on to the start-finish straight as Hill thrust the Williams down the pit lane exit: a tortuous left followed by a dip. Hill reached the bottom of the dip as Senna rounded Turn One.

Hill pressed out on to the circuit, the dry tyres flinging spray, as Senna bore down on him. Senna had the impetus, Senna had nicely warmed tyres and within a couple of corners reeled Hill in, slip-streamed.

'I'd just come out on the slicks,' Hill says, 'and I was a bit cautious. I stayed on a dry line and he had to go down a wet bit. He took a

135

Wet–dry in Brazil, and Senna timed everything perfectly to win from Damon Hill (Williams).

gamble and got away with it. He was through. If I'd had a lap to get up to speed on the slicks . . .'

The Brazilian Grand Prix had been decided, Hill making the mature decision to accept second place. Senna's postview: 'This was one of my best victories, although not as good as 1991. In these conditions you need everything working for you, the whole team, to win. I didn't have a car fast enough to keep up with the Williams but it ran trouble free all the way and to see the crowd . . . that's something you have to experience for yourself'.

'After the race I've never seen anybody so happy,' Ramirez says. 'It was absolutely hilarious. We had a party in one of the discotheques and we were throwing him up in the air and Pele was there and it was . . . fantastic. Ayrton really, really enjoyed that.' Yes, and talked and celebrated so much he had a sore throat for a week and needed antibiotics.

In a car which (theoretically) stood practically no chance Senna led the World Championship with 16 points, Prost 10, Hill and Blundell (Ligier) 6. Still better was to come two weeks later: Ayrton Senna da Silva, son of Milton Guirado Theodoro and Neyde, brother of Viviane and Leonardo, would create one of the greatest laps ever driven and construct upon that one of the greatest victories.

He'd not agreed terms for the season when he journeyed to Donington Park and the European Grand Prix, giving a strange twist to what followed. A predictable, almost inevitable, grid — Prost pole from Hill, Schumacher and Senna on the second row — but England in April offered Senna a chance. On Sunday 11 April rain had fallen on Donington and although it stopped only Lehto (Sauber) risked dry tyres. Senna's thinking as he reached the grid and settled: *I'll really go for it before the Williams have time to settle. Because they hold technical superiority that's the tactic.*

A fast change from red to green, Prost off securely enough, Hill close to Prost, Schumacher mid-track, Wendlinger (Sauber) surging alongside Schumacher then going to mid-track. That elbowed Schumacher who elbowed Senna, forcing him so far that he put two wheels on to the triangle which bisected the grass and the pit lane exit, a triangle painted blue and white and very slippery.

Senna twisted the McLaren back so sharply he went across the track and tried to go inside Schumacher into Redgate, a long horseshoe right. The exact positioning: Prost on the racing line and clear, Hill slotting in. Wendlinger deep to the inside behind Hill, Senna behind Wendlinger, Schumacher coming to the inside; couldn't. Senna already in occupation.

Rounding the second part of the horseshoe Prost moved to mid-track, Hill followed Prost there and Wendlinger followed Hill there, Schumacher still on the outside. It left an open channel *inside*. Senna turned late into that channel, the horseshoe folding from him, two wheels riding the boundary line of the circuit. He'd shed Schumacher.

They travelled downhill to the left-and-right of the Craner Curves, Senna pitching the McLaren *outside* Wendlinger describing an enormous arc.

Third.

'I saw him in the mirrors,' Wendlinger says, 'and I could see the way he was driving. I knew his reputation in the wet and I knew precisely what he was going to do. I decided I'd better leave some room. I didn't want to go out of the race there and then.'

'I will never forget that lap. He'd psyched them out, demoralized the whole lot of them'

This move had to be the limit. Ron Dennis says 'he knew the exact limit of the car and drove aggressively'. What is the limit? As Senna described that arc round Wendlinger we might hear him repeat *knowing your limit is a mental and physical thing. In some conditions it's physical and you just cannot overcome that. In some it's mental because you have to be constant in your mind.*

They travelled up the incline to Starkeys Bridge, a left. Senna caught Hill. Out of Starkeys, Senna came up level but on the *inside*, perfect for McLeans corner, a right. Senna had the McLaren deep to that inside and went through.

Second.

'I made a bad start,' Hill says. 'I'd actually thought I could get ahead of Alain into Redgate and if I had I'd have pushed hard to get away because in the wet the guy behind can't see while the leader has a clear track, although balanced against that is the danger of not knowing exactly how the track will be. I was a bit peeved to be behind Alain, I couldn't really see, and my concern was to stick with him and hopefully we'd pull away from the people following. You can't see what's going on behind you: you certainly see there's a car behind, and you might just make it out as a red car or a white car or something, but you don't know which car until it is alongside. I might have fought the corner but it was very early in the race for a risk like that. When he got past me I thought *for God's sake, Ayrton!* Then I thought *hold him up, Alain. Make sure you don't let him get ahead.*'

Around Coppice, a curving right, Senna gained on Prost. Along Starkeys Straight he gained on Prost, through the Esses — flick-left, flick-right — he caught him. They travelled towards the Melbourne Hairpin, a tight horseshoe. Senna lined the McLaren up mid-track, Prost outside him, and seized the *inside*. Both cars slithered but Senna now seized the hairpin.

First.

Lap one: Senna 1:35.843
            Prost 1:36.541
            Hill 1:36.963

Of the millions of laps driven since the modern era of the World Championship began in 1950, no-one can or ever will know which is the best. It is too immense and subjective a matter. But no-one can reasonably doubt that the one minute 35.843 seconds is a candidate.

Ramirez, in the pits, says 'I will never forget that lap. He'd psyched them out, demoralized the whole lot of them. He won the whole race on that first lap. I saw him go by in the lead and I thought *it can't possibly be. How can it be? How can he have that advantage? The Williamses must be on dry tyres.* I watched and no, they were on wet tyres, same as us. I knew how good Ayrton is — we all know how good Ayrton is — superman in the wet, how he has a lot more feeling than most other drivers in the wet and our car was perfect for the wet conditions but even so . . .'

Lap two: Senna 1:27.882
            Prost 1:31.429
            Hill 1:32.003

'I began to think maybe I'd been mistaken about the tyres on the

Williamses,' Ramirez says. 'Second lap I ran to the pit lane wall but no mistake, wet tyres same as us. I was still thinking *how can this guy have this incredible advantage?* I believe Williams had problems with the gear-shift. Changing down they were locking the back wheels, meaning their cars were very difficult to drive but even so . . .'

> Lap three: Senna 1:28.203
>   Prost 1:30.722
>   Hill 1:30.908

The order solidified — Rubens Barrichello (Jordan) an inspired fourth, then Alesi, then Schumacher. This order endured to lap 16 when Alesi pitted for slicks, Hill and Schumacher a lap later. Senna a lap after that, Prost a lap after that. Order: Senna, Prost, Hill, Alesi, Barrichello, Schumacher, all on dries. Because the lap charts will assume surreal proportions, pock-marked by pit stops in bewildering profusion — so many that the Williams team *ran out of new tyres* — it is worth breaking the narrative at lap 20 to examine the philosophy of the pit stop.

The emotion of victory, supporters streaming towards the McLaren.

Dennis is McLaren's man in control. He stands on the pit lane wall. He wears headphones and can hear and speak to the driver. He has computer screens in front of him, giving times. He says, 'You are in a unique position compared to the driver who, and I use a slight over-simplification, can only see the car in front and the car behind. You have a complete view of the race, you can see — taking Donington — what lap times other cars are achieving based on their tyre choice. You can see the traffic your driver will be coming up to. It enables you to choose the time for a pit stop and have a strategic input into the race. I pick a team that is well-disciplined and utilizes the technology and, taking it together, it can significantly influence the outcome of a Grand Prix.

'With the driver there is continuous dialogue backwards and forwards. The driver is always in a better position to understand what is going on with the tyres than the people on the pit lane wall — he is in the car. Inevitably, however, there is information available to us — like at Adelaide, 1993 (another story of pit stops) — where we place greater pressure on the driver to stop. In that situation at Adelaide the team over-ruled the driver and instructed him to stop. Of course, all drivers do as they are told (smile) but sometimes it takes a couple of laps to impress on them the importance of stopping'.

The times, lap 20:

Senna	29m 45.973
Prost	at 5.141
Hill	at 6.913
Alesi	at 16.445
Barrichello	at 19.876
Schumacher	at 20.495

The race might have been plucked from Senna on lap 21. Through Coppice he came upon Fittipaldi and Blundell scrapping among themselves. Down Starkeys Straight Blundell moved out to take Fittipaldi at the instant Senna moved out to take *him*. Blundell reached the flick-left of the Esses but his momentum took him fast-forward and off. Fittipaldi, seeing Blundell go, twitched left into the mouth of the Esses and found Senna already there. Senna went on to the kerbing and they nudged wheels.

'Yes. I was scrapping with Fittipaldi,' Blundell says. 'It was one of

American Michael Andretti had joined McLaren in place of Berger and had a wretched season. He didn't complete a lap in the European Grand Prix at Donington.

those races where conditions were poor but it started to dry. There was only one dry line. Unbeknown to me Senna sat behind us, making us into a little trio. I made my manoeuvre to go by Fittipaldi, Senna ducking and diving trying to go by the pair of us. I went on to the damp patch of the circuit and, to be brutal about it, went in too deep and couldn't gather it all up. I had to continue straight on: no adhesion. Only at that point, when I was stationary sitting there in the cockpit, did I see Senna going through. I suppose he had to slow up somewhat anyway because Fittipaldi would have been in a bit of a state.

'Drivers do keep tabs on what is going on. You do look in your mirrors for an amount of the time but when you're scrapping at 180mph to 200mph the level of concentration and effort has to go up another level: you're calculating the element of risk. You calculate the weak points of the other car, you calculate the car-and-driver package, where you think you can take them. That might last for a couple of laps. If there is someone behind you, or a pack behind you, with a big speed differential they'll soon be on you. And there was a big differential with Senna, as we saw when he just went off into the distance from the first lap. Things come on top of you within seconds so you can't always be 100 per cent on top of it.'

Raindrops fell, plump and getting plumper. Prost pitted for wets on lap 22, Hill two laps later, to steal an advantage over Senna — but this might be dangerous. How wet would the track be in another five minutes, 10, 20? How dry? England in April, remember. Senna on the roulette wheel was staying with dries as the drizzle hardened to rain. Advantage Prost? No.

	Senna	Prost	Hill
Lap 24	1:26.363	1:27.015	1:30.772
Lap 25	1:26.210	1:26.552	1:47.749
			(after his stop)
Lap 26	1:26.365	1:27.720	1:27.249
Lap 27	1:26.249	1:27.291	1:28.607
Lap 28	1:27.617	1:26.441	1:27.706

You can almost hear the continuous dialogue backwards and forwards. *Prost's just done a quicker lap than you Ayrton*, even though the order had become Senna, Alesi, Prost, Barrichello, Hill, Herbert. Senna held a lead of more than 20 seconds over Alesi, more than 30 seconds over Prost. By staying out, Senna had established enough of a lead to pit and retain the lead — and Alesi would have to stop soon too. The rain eased to drizzle but Senna pitted for wets on lap 28 — and did retain the lead.

	Senna	Prost	Hill
Lap 30	1:28.789	1:27.040	1:28.827
Lap 31	1:29.433	1:26.221	1.30.219
Lap 32	1:27.562	1:25.544	1:29.625

Order: Senna, Prost, Barrichello, Hill, Alesi, Herbert. On lap 33, the track drying, Prost gambled and pitted for dries, and a lap later Senna followed. It cost him the lead. 'Something went wrong on the right rear-wheel but those guys are really under pressure. It's motor racing.' A wheelnut cross-threaded, holding Senna stationary for 20 seconds. Prost led by some seven seconds.

And the rain returned. It forced Prost to pit for wets on lap 38, Hill on lap 41. Senna stayed out, balancing his skill against the weather, the McLaren dancing a bit but never out of overall control. It was a master at work at the crux of a race.

	Senna	Prost	Hill
Lap 42	1:25.686	1:28.293	1:45.381
Lap 43	1:26.460	1:26.119	1:25.260
Lap 44	1:24.166	1:26.503	1:25.359

By lap 46 Senna had dipped into the one minute 23s, Prost at the one minute 27s, the track drying. Prost had to gamble again or lose the race. He pitted for dries on lap 48 and stalled, the clutch misbehaving. Order when it re-settled: Senna, Barrichello, Hill; then Prost, Herbert and Patrese (Benetton) a lap down. On lap 53 Prost pitted for the sixth time to change his left rear. He'd felt a puncture. Barrichello pitted on lap 55, so Senna led the European Grand Prix by a lap. 'Ayrton and the team worked well,' Ramirez says. 'We did less pit stops than the others so we were gaining time and when he

Tom Wheatcroft, owner of Donington, long dreamed of a Grand Prix – and got a great one. This race was wet–dry–wet–dry and Senna was supreme.

led by a lap it was unbelievable, unbelievable.'

And the rain came back. Senna entered the pit lane for wets, ran urgently down the pit lane, waved a gloved hand at the pit crew and — kept on! 'I was calling on the radio "wets, wets, wets" and I came in but the crew weren't ready. I could see them wheeling the tyres from the garage so I went back out.' Forgive the crew. It was the only moment of disharmony in this improbable, incomparable afternoon. Mind you, by entering the pits you avoided going all the way round Goddards: a considerable economy.

Senna's pit lane run gave him fastest lap of the race, something unique and surreal of itself.

Senna covered another lap and decided to stay out 'to see if I could hang on', but Hill unlapped himself. Senna pitted for wets on lap 66 — 'the rain got worse and I had to come in'. Hill and Prost responded by pitting themselves but by now the team had no more new sets and had to fit used ones. Forgive them. Hill changed on laps 17, 24, 34, 41, 50 and 68. Prost on 19, 22, 33, 38, 48, 53 and this lap of 69.

In the gathering murk Senna eased across the final few laps, the rain harder. The full magnitude of his achievement:

Senna	1h 50m 46.570
Hill	at 1m 23.199
Prost	at one lap
Herbert	at one lap
Patrese	at two laps
Barbazza	at two laps

Dennis: 'Donington was one of the best strategic races we have ever had, one where we were in complete harmony'.

Ramirez: 'After that race Ayrton felt ever so well. He loved it, he really enjoyed it. It's a race he will talk about himself for ever'.

Senna that afternoon: 'I don't know how many times we stopped for tyres (slow smile). I thing it's surely the record in any race. Driving with slicks in damp and very slippery conditions was a tremendous effort because you just don't get the feeling from the car, you have to commit yourself to certain corners and you can be off the circuit. Conditions like this is gambling and it's taking chances that pay off and we gambled well. I feel very light about it all. I wish I could go home and have another party like Brazil. Then I would have

At Imola Senna kept Prost at bay for six laps.

another week of bad throat and antibiotics but I would go through it
again. We won as a group. So many things happened that I find it
hard to remember'. Subsequently Senna would add to this. 'That race
told me everything to myself. It was what I wanted to prove to
myself.'

Brundle: 'That performance was simply incredible. It required not
only technique and nerve but brain'.

It brings us back to the chilly day in Estoril, January 1994, Senna
in reflective mood. 'A natural tendency for a driver, as long as he is
able to do his job with a team, is to learn continuously. Experience
only adds to your driving, provided you can keep your motivation at a
single level. I think that's the case almost every year of my career
from 1984, always just a little bit better — not necessarily faster but
more consistent, less susceptible to mistakes, thinking always, always,
always. That experience allows you to be a step ahead all the time,
ready to make the next move in a race.'

Like at Donington three pit stops ahead?

'Whatever . . .'

On the grey and dank evening of 11 April 1993 the World

Championship against every probability, stood at Senna 26 points, Prost 14, Hill 12. Without (I hope) being presumptuous, I sent Senna a fax shortly after this: *Thinking is the best way to travel.*

Would Senna sign for McLaren for the rest of the season? At Donington he didn't want to talk about that and the waiting game went on. He did, however, begin to put pressure on Ford who were contracted to supplying Benetton with 'premium' engines. 'It is a ridiculous situation that Ford is in with us. Ford's only chance to win Grands Prix is with McLaren. Benetton may win a race but only if Williams and McLaren drop out. Ford has two Grand Prix victories and is leading the Championship after three races with a car which is still under-developed and an engine which is recognised as being half a second to a second down on the other specification Ford engine.'

Senna continued the pressure at Imola after negotiations between Ford, Benetton and McLaren broke down. He accused Benetton of making demands which had been met and then altering the demands. (Senna's and McLaren's pressure paid off eventually and they had the engines for the British Grand Prix at Silverstone.)

He'd arrived at Imola from Brazil five minutes before Friday's untimed practice and spun, spun in first qualifying, spun again in second qualifying but put the McLaren on the second row. A wet race (fourth out of four), Hill leading and spinning, Prost leading and Senna following until, after 42 laps, the McLaren suffered a 'hydraulic failure at the end of the straight at over 300kph. It was close. I managed to stop the car and shortly after I lost all systems'. Prost won.

In Spain Senna qualified on the second row and, after muscular movements around Turn One, Prost led from Hill, Senna third. He couldn't stay with either Williams but — can you hear, Ford? — Schumacher, initially close, couldn't stay with him. The core of the Grand Prix became Prost stalking Hill and taking him, Senna running third to lap 42 when Hill's engine failed. Senna inherited and stayed second despite a late pit stop. 'I came in because the rear tyres in particular were worn and dirty and affecting the balance of the car. It's better to stop and be safe — though it was an unusual stop!' The left rear stuck, holding him stationary for 15.01 seconds.

'I had several big moments with traffic. People's engines blew up in front of me two or three times and the last time I got my visor full of

147

oil. That was five, six laps from the end and I had a tremendously big problem just to see. When I tried to clean the visor I couldn't get clear visibility. Schumacher pushed hard so I just tried to stay in front of him.' Prost 34, Senna 32, Schumacher 14, Hill 12.

Prost took pole from Schumacher at Monaco. Senna second row *but directly behind Prost*, despite an accident. 'It was caused by some bumps at the exit to the tunnel. The car didn't handle them too well and I lost it. More than a crash it was a scratch. My hand hurts but I'm only aware of it when there is a kickback from the wheel, when I'm on the kerb, for example.'

'The shunt made me lose my edge a bit . . . I knew I'd be in for a very rough race'

At the start Prost crept a fraction before the green light and took the lead — he'd be penalized with a 10 second stop-go for the crawling but not yet — Schumacher and Senna following. The hand proved 'a problem because the difference between going flat out at Monaco or only at 90 per cent is crucial. The shunt made me lose my edge a bit. When I couldn't make the front row I knew I'd be in for a very rough race'.

His thinking: *I thought it through the night before. I knew I couldn't take the lead. I had to cope with the speed of the Williams so I hoped that their tyre wear would be worse than mine. Prost jumped the start, perhaps in desperation to get to the first corner, a result of the pressure I exerted even though I was behind him. Things went my way but I had a plan and I stuck to it.*

Prost's stop-go, compounded by his stalling twice trying to accelerate from it, deposited him twenty second. Schumacher, maturing, led comfortably but on lap 33 the hydraulics failed. Senna made no mistake for the rest of the race and that was his sixth Monaco win. (This total beat the record of five set by Hill's father Graham between 1963 and 1969.) Senna 42, Prost 37, Hill 18, Schumacher 14.

The splendour of Senna would be demonstrated in Canada, a dry race, and he couldn't hope for another Donington first lap. That does not diminish what he did do.

Prost

Hill

Schumacher

Patrese

Berger

Alesi

Brundle

Senna

At the green the twin columns inter-weaved, Berger taking his Ferrari to midtrack instantly, Alesi taking his Ferrari to mid-track behind Berger — Schumacher hadn't started cleanly. They moulded to one column, Hill, Prost, Berger, Alesi, Patrese, Senna. Into the first left-hander, 90 degrees, Senna went *outside* Patrese. Some 50 metres ahead a right-horseshoe uncoiled. Senna's outside translated to the *inside* for that but Alesi and Patrese, both feeling for the racing line — *inside* — engulfed him. Picture this: the broad red and white kerbing in its uncoiling, Senna sandwiched full on to it, all four wheels. He kept his acceleration on the kerbing so that while Alesi went ahead Senna ran abreast with Patrese.

Out of the horseshoe he ran wheel to wheel with Patrese and passed him. Quickly, quickly he caught Alesi, tracked him, a great impetus growing. At the hairpin he went *outside* Alesi and now they ran wheel to wheel, almost touched out of the hairpin. Into the next left Senna held the inside, Alesi mid track. And now their wheels were so close you could scarcely see a sliver of daylight between them. Senna muscled Alesi on the run to the chicane before the pits, fled past him, the impetus still growing. On lap 2 it brought him up to Berger and he took Berger at the hairpin on the *inside*.

Deep into the race Hill's pit stop went wrong. This left Senna second to Prost until, only seven laps left, the electrics expired. 'The car suddenly started cutting out.'

Before the French Grand Prix, Senna did commit himself to McLaren for the rest of the season but in that race the Championship began to drift from him. Prost won, Senna fourth. Prost 57, Senna 45, Hill 28, Schumacher 24. Silverstone would not forgive any car with less power than the Williams. Worse, McLaren ran a lot of wing to solve what Senna described as 'stability problems, but of course this slowed us down the straights'.

Senna slogs on in Spain, but he can't catch Prost.

Prost blew the start at Silverstone and found himself third behind Senna. The moves and counter-moves after that were frankly alarming, the cars flicking towards each other at full bore, flicking apart and at one moment Prost had to hammer the brakes to avoid the McLaren. I happened to be watching with Nigel Roebuck of *Autosport*. We held our breaths and didn't speak, Roebuck reaching for words and not initially finding any. Then he almost gabbled *and what speed are they doing, what speed are they doing? J-e-s-u-s.*

There's a borderline between impetus, maximizing a Formula 1 car and refusing to concede a struggle with a car behind. This was as close to crossing the borderline as you'd want to witness: a communal relief greeted Prost getting safely past, a handful of laps later. Prost told Roebuck 'It was very difficult and sometimes very dangerous but I don't want to say more than that. There's no point'.

Senna ran out of fuel with a lap left, to be classified fifth — Prost 67, Senna 47, Schumacher 30, Hill 28.

Senna the maximizer in Germany, also. Prost blew the start again — Hill leading from Schumacher — and Prost and Senna disputed possession of the first chicane in a male way. 'Alain and I both braked very late. I don't know if we touched but we were both beyond our limit. I lost control and spun off.' To which Prost said 'it was very close. If I hadn't gone wide we'd have touched. It doesn't happen very often but I decided I was not going to back off this time'.

Senna, twenty fourth after the spin and nothing to lose, mounted a power play on the Hockenheimring and he became another Ayrton Senna now — all poise and finesse, disciplined, carving space to overtake. There were no teeth-grinding moves and counter-moves, no border-line, *completely different from Silverstone and Prost.*

By lap 2 he'd reached twentieth, by lap 5 fifteenth, by lap 14 seventh, by lap 27 sixth. He'd make one of his prudent late stops for tyres — 'the car felt funny and the last thing I want is to risk a blow-out at 300kph'. He finished fourth, and scant consolation in that. Hill ought to have won but did have a blow-out a couple of laps from the end, giving the 10 points to Prost. The Championship: Prost 77, Senna 50, Schumacher 36, Hill 28.

Hill won Hungary. Senna was a strong second until lap 18 when the electrics expired. 'I could have taken Hill on the second corner but I decided on a more cautious approach because the car felt near

Images of Monaco: the power and the precision – and a win because Prost had a stop-go penalty for jumping the start.

its limit. Quite soon I started to experience problems with the throttle. This affected my control and on some bends I felt like a passenger. I tried to re-set the electronics but that caused the engine to misfire and the throttle to behave worse.'

Two aspects of Senna at Spa. In an interview with Joe Saward of *Autosport* Senna said: 'There is an area where logic applies and another where it does not. No matter how far down the road you are in understanding and experiencing religion there are certain things which we cannot logically explain. We tend always to understand only what we can see, the colours, the touch and the smell. If it is outside that, is it crazy? I had the great opportunity to experience something beyond that. Once you have experienced it, you know it is there and that is why you have to tell people'.

In qualifying, the Lotus of Alessandro Zanardi snapped out of control breasting Eau Rouge at 150mph (240kph) and beat into the barrier, rose, and went wildly the width of the track into the other barrier spraying bits everywhere. Andretti came upon this and slowed, feeling for a path through the debris. Senna, coming very

Senna got as high as second in Canada but the alternator failed. He was classified eighteenth.

hard upon this, struck some debris. His mind moved clinically and decisively. His thinking: *I saw Michael at 45 degrees to the racing line. I had nowhere to go and I knew I couldn't stop the car completely because of the debris and sand. I had to choose a way of avoiding another accident, avoiding Zanardi's car and all the marshals on the circuit.*

Senna pitched his car sideways, the front right tyre leaving a black scar along the track. Two of the marshals attending Zanardi glimpsed Senna and ran for their lives. Senna missed Andretti's rear by centimetres and struck the armco still sideways. The car stopped within a couple of metres of the marshals who hadn't run. The range of reflexes of the racing driver, the thought-processes of the racing driver are quite different from those of other people. His thinking: *When I saw that Zanardi was OK I put the incident out of my mind completely.*

The stewards, however, reprimanded Senna for not slowing under yellow warning flags . . .

An unforgiving Belgian Grand Prix, no opportunity for Senna to apply mind games, think a victory. What Senna could do, and did do, was ravish the start from the third row, *outside* Alesi, *outside* Hill at La

Source to be second behind Prost. Hill used the power of Renault on lap 2 and went by up the incline to Les Combes.

Schumacher, hobbled on the start line by a systems failure, charged and reached Senna, who'd say 'the first few laps were fun but then I just could not keep up the pace. I stopped early for tyres (lap 13) because I felt that would give me the best chance to fight with Schumacher'. Schumacher came second, Prost third and Senna fourth. Prost 81, Senna 53, Hill 48, Schumacher 42.

To understand the start at Monza, where Prost could take the Championship, you need to understand Senna's predicament. At high speed circuits and if no rain fell he couldn't hope to run with either Williams *but*, using his abilities he could take an initial advantage, perhaps even lead, and see what happened next. He phrased it himself. 'Reliability, balance and a good start are essential.' The only other tactic would have been to hang back and hope the Williams crashed or broke down. If they didn't he'd be at best third. It was not inside Ayrton Senna to accept third place in any Grand Prix before it had started.

Prost

Hill

Alesi

Senna

For once, Prost started well. Alesi thrust towards Prost, Senna positioned behind Alesi. It placed Hill to the right as they stampeded to the first chicane, a hard-left-right. A hundred metres from the chicane, Alesi had nosed ahead of Hill, Senna following. Into the mouth, Hill and Senna were parallel, Senna on the *inside*. They turned in and touched, Senna briefly airborne. Senna bounded through the chicane on to the grass but kept the engine running and rejoined tenth. 'Alesi and I both took Hill but he insisted on trying to stay on the outside. It was quite a hit but I landed more or less in the right direction.'

He went to lap 9 and thumped into the back of Brundle. 'We both late-braked. The rear of the car had been feeling light under braking for a while and when I came up to Martin I just could not hold it. I was very close to him and without downforce the car lacked grip at the rear. Under the braking I lost it and hit him.'

Prost ought to have won but the engine failed near the end. The confirmation of the Championship shifted on to Portugal where Prost

155

The alarming, yet electrifying duel with Prost at Silverstone.

took it, calculating each of his moves and counter-moves: he nibbled at and dabbled with Schumacher for the lead, didn't get it and was happy to finish second. It was enough. Senna himself ran second early on before 'the engine suddenly blew with a big bang. I really feared it might catch fire'. In Portugal, Prost announced his retirement, insisting he'd long been contemplating it. The door opened for Senna.

In Japan, Irvine made his debut in a Jordan and qualified well, the fourth row. Senna took the lead and held it until lap 21 when he pitted for tyres, regained it when Prost pitted. This was a wet-dry race and after the mid-point Senna, on wets, came up to Irvine and Hill squabbling over fifth place. Senna moved past Irvine, also on wets, but although he drew up to Hill couldn't overtake. Irvine decided to unlap himself and nipped past Senna, to Senna's surprise and intense anger. Irvine now traded places with Hill, nervy and raw combat, Senna staying a little way back. Senna readied himself and sliced by Irvine again, sliced by Hill. The anger did not dissipate.

He pitted for slicks, an unplanned stop but 'we had heavy tyre wear and I knew I couldn't have held Prost (in second place) in the later laps'. Senna won.

He contained the anger for the duration of the televised Press Conference, let it simmer rather than boil over although you could sense his animation. 'I had lots of scary moments with back-markers, just very unprofessional. If you are leading the race it shouldn't happen that a guy makes life so difficult for you to overtake for two, three, five laps — and then when you overtake and the guy in front of him makes a mistake and you slow down, the other guy is coming behind you hitting you, banging the wheels and *I am leading the race. I am lapping people.* Very unprofessional. I think measures should be taken against drivers like that.'

What followed remains awkward to accommodate. Senna strode to the Jordan office in the paddock to explain Formula 1 etiquette to Eddie Irvine. As he spoke the anger did rise — and rise, the cadence of his voice rising, too. He stabbed in the f-word again and again. A racing impetus governed him. Irvine defended his corner in a trenchant way, conceding nothing and asking 'did I touch you? Did I touch you once?' It culminated in Senna cuffing him and being escorted out of the office.

To cuff another driver is not a defensible position, as Senna would acknowledge. But it did illustrate a naked passion for what he regarded as fair play, for right and wrong — a passion so profound that expressing it took him into the wrong himself.

For a calm, external view I turned to Mark Blundell. 'There are morals involved in our sport, when the leader is behind you, for instance. You should give him a little bit of lee-way to get through. On the flip side of that, you are there doing your own race, especially if you're fighting with another car when the leader does come up to you. And the leader was in your position at one stage of his career. The flip side also involves this: you get back to the pits and the team manager gives you a bollocking for losing time because letting the leader go through cost you that time.'

What if he's leading and you come up to him to unlap yourself and you're going a lot faster?

'At that point the brain has to engage gear and take all things into consideration, weigh it up, but I'd say 95 per cent of the time you would have to go by the leader if you were quicker. If you sat behind him for three or four laps and if he wasn't under pressure in the race he'd probably let you go by anyway because you are only going to

And he would, very soon. This is Hungary.

interfere with him. Where Irvine went wrong was that Ayrton was looking for a way past Hill and couldn't find it and Irvine took the chance to pass Ayrton. If Ayrton had been behind Hill for five laps and couldn't get past because manifestly he wasn't quick enough to do it, Irvine could have thought *these blokes are holding me up*, and that's a different thing.'

At the other level, the racing level, Ramirez gives an illustration of what Senna had. Andretti departed Formula 1 before Portugal, allowing McLaren to field their third driver, Hakkinen, and he outqualified Senna (one minute 12.443 against one minute 12.491). 'When Gerhard Berger was with us Ayrton was quicker because he had the ability to concentrate not just for a qualifying lap but lap after lap in a race. Mika was quicker in qualifying in Portugal, then we go to Japan, a much more difficult circuit. Ayrton had the edge in qualifying though Mika went well (one minute 37.284 against one minute 37.326).

'Ayrton won the race and Mika came third but the difference between the two was over 25 seconds. After the race Mika seemed a little down and I asked "did you have any problems?" He said "no, the car was perfect". You could see through his mind that he knew the difference between himself and Ayrton: that Ayrton could do a lap in qualifying and then do it again in the race, lap after lap after lap, and that translated to the 25 seconds.'

Australia carried an echo of that word concentration. Senna took pole, his only one of the season, in the first session. 'Had there been no traffic I could have done better. We also had a problem with the radio. I was wondering whether I should come in because of low fuel. I wasn't getting a reply so I was shouting, especially as I neared the pit entrance. Later I discovered that my radio button was stuck, so the pits couldn't talk back to me. The result was that I could not concentrate in the usual way and so I couldn't improve my time.'

He returned to the subject of Irvine, eyes ablaze. 'Nothing justifies hitting him and I'm not justifying myself, I'm just saying what took place in the race was absurd in many different ways. And nobody did anything about it, or even talked about it, during or after the race. I went to see him and he was like a wall. He made me lose my temper. I couldn't help it because respect is very important between drivers. The problem was he wouldn't even think about it, let alone say he was wrong. And the people round him were not in a normal state.

Hill won Spa, Senna fourth.

They were drunk and no-one did anything to prevent what occurred. They all stood there looking cynical. When the leader comes, even if you are World Champion, you must make way. That is the code of conduct between us and it has been like that since I started racing.'

(You might ponder what Senna said before the Portuguese Grand Prix, 1984, and wonder why, with the World Championship in play, he insisted he wouldn't melt out of Niki Lauda's path. The answer? Senna qualified third, Lauda eleventh, so that when Lauda did come upon him *Lauda would not be in the lead but moving up through the field.* Across the years in between we'd seen Senna do all manner of things on race tracks but never, as far as I can recall, hamper the leader from lowly positions. Interesting . . .)

He found the moments before the start at Adelaide, his last race for McLaren, 'incredibly tough. I had to keep my feelings very much under control because in those moments the emotions were taking over. The last half hour was very hard — these emotions kept coming back, making me feel very uneasy. I wanted to do the best for the team and myself. I had to win the race. That is why I had to keep my emotions under control'. Ramirez — who Senna senses is also

A moment of calm, almost a moment of pelmanism before Senna won the Japanese Grand Prix.

emotional — came near him two or three times with the minutes ticking and Senna 'couldn't cope'.

Ramirez says 'yes I was emotional and it was sad. I tried not to think it will be the last time'. Nor can it have helped that Ramirez said he'd forgive him for leaving if he won the race.

With no more than five minutes left Senna started the process of clearing his mind. On the grid before the parade lap he sat as we have seen him sit on so many grids before but not, this once, withdrawing into himself, eyes locked straight ahead gazing from another dimension. His head moved from side to side, absorbing the swell of movement around the car, the mechanics doing a final fine-tuning, Ron Dennis walking up to ensure all was well. Senna's eyes seemed reddened . . .

He led virtually the whole race and pitted six laps earlier than Prost. Echoing Donington, Ron Dennis says 'that was another very good strategic race where the whole team performed well and contributed a lot'. The backwards and forwards at Adelaide: a discussion, then Senna radios 'now!' and Dennis sets the crew in motion for the stop. Senna won the Australian Grand Prix from Prost by nine seconds.

He drove down the pit lane holding a Brazilian flag, the victory lap completed, and a phalanx of marshals kept the crowd at bay while he turned into the McLaren pit for the last time. Dennis waited there. Senna climbed out of the car and they embraced, Senna patting Dennis's back, then his head. McLaren had now won more races than Ferrari: 104 to 103. Senna made a tour of the McLaren team-members, shaking the hand of each, sometimes embracing them, patting Hakkinen. Tears might have welled at any instant.

He discussed the leaving, eyes hooded into sadness. 'The most important thing is to keep the good moments and keep the happiness we had together. I had a tremendous time. The record speaks for itself, the results, the Championships and I got respect from the people I worked with so long. I have tremendous respect for them as well. I am leaving friends behind. I think that's the best way to do it, leaving friends behind.'

There's a postscript, or more properly a pre-Adelaide postscript.

Blundell wouldn't be staying with Ligier and, with the return of Prost to McLaren no more than surmise, he sought out Senna for advice. 'Ayrton was on the same plane to Australia, we were up the front end, I strolled over and we had a good chat, 35 or 40 minutes. I picked his brains, picked his brains, picked his brains on how he thought I should handle the situation. He was very helpful, very, very helpful.'

Blundell's options: try for McLaren and risk becoming the third driver if Prost did return — namely test driver again — or try for the best team he could get as a regular driver.

'Let me say that Ayrton is an outstanding race driver and he also has an outstanding brain. When the day comes that he finally puts the steering wheel to one side and turns that brain 100 per cent to business he will create a massive impact. He thought about my situation, thought what was available to Ron Dennis and expressed the opinion that I'd have a very good chance of getting the McLaren drive: Ron knew me from testing in 1992, knew the way I work. Ayrton pointed out that the Prost situation would always be at the forefront and he took that into consideration. If that dies down, he judged, I'd stand a good chance. I appreciated that very sincerely.'

CHAPTER SIX

Cries From The Heart

In many ways we are a dream for people, not a reality. That counts in your mind. It shows how much you can touch people, and as much as you can try to give those people something it is nothing compared to what they live in their own mind, in their dreams, for you. And that is something really special, something really, really special for me. — Ayrton Senna

People in the outside world don't know me and make assumptions, wrong assumptions. — Ayrton Senna

THESE WORDS PENETRATE territory rarely discussed or dissected, presumably since it is taken for granted. Curious. Part of a public performer is what he does, part is what he is and part is the effect — impact, if you like — on those who watch. A ballet critic will convey the emotional effect of a performance naturally and unselfconsciously as an integral part of the experience. Sports critics don't often do that, preferring self-consciously to hint towards it, because they're writing about a competition played out to rules and producing winners and losers. A ballet critic would have done an interesting job on Senna's first lap at Donington.

When the first edition of *The Hard Edge of Genius* appeared I received an array of letters from readers struggling to express their dreams and realities of Ayrton Senna. All were from women. Some were straightforward fan letters, others profound and veering in totally unexpected directions.

Most sport is reported by men for men. That leads to a paradox: women constitute a goodly proportion of the attendance at major events and (as it would seem from the letters) view what they see from the unexpected directions. A man following a Rugby League team may delight in — or despair of — what that team does, a woman following the same team may, too, while simultaneously seeing the players as virility, as stags rutting.

'I don't think the phenomenon of attraction to racing drivers has ever been satisfactorily analysed'

The sexuality of sport is as little reported as the effect sports people have on their audiences, presumably for the same reason. Some players are highly aware of the effect — Andre Agassi at Wimbledon bearing his chest to change shirts between games and knowing a reverberating feminine shriek will accompany it. That Agassi may be able to make total strangers sitting high up in a grandstand have palpitations (or more extreme sensations) really isn't the sort of thing a *chap* reporting Wimbledon would want to know about, is it? But how can you fully understand Agassi and Wimbledon and the nature of tennis if you don't?

Take golf, which you'd think was stately, pure and scarcely erotic. Yet groupies exist even there. Rick Ross, coach to the American golfer John Daly, says 'I have seen women spectators remove their panties and sit in his eye-line as he prepares to putt'. And I haven't mentioned the rutting of boxing, the climax of a goal in football, the jockey *riding and whipping* a horse to win, win, win, or that horse riding can excite some women.

The woman's view of Formula 1 has not, as far as I am aware, ever been reported except in the sense of women journalists interviewing drivers' wives/girlfriends and raking over very familiar territory, *how do you cope with the danger? Can you bear to watch your husband? What does he eat before the races?* The answers cover familiar territory, too. I *worry but I try not to let him see I'm worried.* This is invariably accompanied by posed photographs portraying normal family life — sofas and gardens are favourite venues.

Over the years I've written biographies of Mansell, Prost, Hunt, Mike Hailwood and Berger and received letters from men expressing this view or that, concentrated around the racing. Only one letter came from a woman, because she happened to be in the background of a photograph. No letter penetrated the territory which the following Senna letters covered.

This chapter is not about overt sex but undercurrents which have gender as their theme. Here are the women speaking for themselves about Senna and if you're a man reading it and feel a voyeur, tough. This is the way it is for *them*. I only ask you to appreciate the theme.

Lyn Patey of Bath:
'The guy is my hero — totally. I was one of the lucky ones who met him several times in 1983 in Formula 3 and who felt that strange sense of pride and loss when he moved up and away from us to

'OK, there are lots of references to speed and the danger adding their own glamour.'

Formula 1. You know, we never could analyse why he provoked such intense emotions in us. He is "only" a racing driver after all. Back home he is probably just like any other rich, attractive young man who happens to be very famous, but bring him back to racing and he becomes magical, mystically special.'

In a letter three years later Ms. Patey expanded:

'I don't think the phenomenon of attraction to racing drivers has ever been satisfactorily analysed. Okay, there are lots of references to speed and the danger adding their own glamour, but obviously there is much more than that. Many women I have talked to have admitted that they find the drivers most attractive when in full race suit and helmet. Kitted up like that the proportions of the figure change: the body in the romper suit and the much enlarged head take on the proportions of a very young child. Hence the cold adrenalin surge of maternal (or paternal) protectiveness when you see someone you care about, for whatever reason, dressed like that and climbing into a race car.'

(The matter of uniforms is a topic of itself, men and air hostesses and so forth, and it can work in reverse. Once upon a time a French racing driver — now no longer alive — found an amour who insisted on making love at the track but only if he wore his racing overalls.)

'Of course the maternal aspect changes once they are in the car. Then they become the ideal man — strapped down, all eyes and no mouth! For me, control is the greatest force. I get a tremendous buzz out of being close to the cars. I find them uncompromisingly, almost painfully, beautiful. The McLaren MP 4/5 brought me out in the biggest goose bumps, and that was before it was fired up.

'So the machines are magnificent. They are capable of speeds beyond my imagination and are also capable of the most terrifying violence. Any man who can control such a beast becomes unimaginably glamorous. Admiration almost becomes worship. The uniform of control, the race suit, automatically raises a man into the ranks of the very special, warranting a second look from the merely mortal.

'The phenomenon is not confined to race drivers either. Sitting next to the driver of an InterCity 225 as we travelled at 125 mph I became aware of a similar effect. Here was this young man, dressed in British Rail shirt and tie and black levis, casually and confidently controlling an enormous machine with the lives of 300 people in his hands. The whole experience was most stimulating — not particularly glamorous in the accepted sense of the word but very impressive. Control is the key and I am very demanding.

'While I have admiration for anyone who can get a race car round a track and return it in one piece, some are rendered very special by the magnitude of their skill — the amount of control exhibited — and it doesn't matter what formula they are in.

'The emotion generated by the success of someone you support is incredible. In 1992 I was working with a Formula 3 class B team and our driver, Hilton Cowie, actually led a race at Thruxton for three mind-bending laps. He eventually finished third overall after his tyres went off. As we were walking back to the truck after the prize-giving I told him he had made me feel like no other man had ever made me feel. Well, it was nearly true! We were all flattened by euphoria because it was our team and it was our little bit of history being made, but that was a one-off and Ayrton has made me feel like that often.

'it must be difficult having the constant pressure . . . He is let's face it, one of the world's best-known people'

'Other than in tragic circumstances no other driver has prompted tears. Monaco 1992 comes particularly to mind because I was watching from the inside of the chicane. There was a splendid photo in *Auto Hebdo* (the French magazine), taken from above. Senna is coming through followed by Mansell and only a cigarette paper separates them. Many of the crowd are gesticulating in excitement and behind the barrier is a figure in a pink jacket with her fists all but rammed into her mouth with the tension — lap chart completely abandoned. I felt foolish later as I walked back round the harbour in front of that huge crowd and realised that I was grinning like an idiot with tears messing up my mascara. That kind of adrenalin rush is certainly addictive and I suspect it would be the same even if I had never met Ayrton.

'One incident that brought home to me the pressure he is under took place in Monaco in 1991. I was walking past the McLaren trucks when I was stopped by the sight of a human whirlpool moving towards me. At the very centre was a small blue cap, its owner flanked by a burly McLaren minder. All around him were screaming women and cheering men, buffeting and pushing him. As the maelstrom reached the nearest truck the minder climbed the steps to the door, reached down and grabbed his driver by his racesuit collar.

'In one fluid movement he heaved Senna up the steps and hurled him through the door into the truck and slammed the door behind him. The minder then stood in front of the door prising away the fingers of dozens of Japanese women who were breaking their finger nails trying to force that door open while other men and women were pounding on the side of the truck shouting "Sen-na, Sen-na". It was terrifying and it was then that I really realised how far he had come from Formula 3. I felt deeply sorry for him.'

Film stars and every transient pop idol will recognise this instantly. Agassi would. So would any Ferrari driver (whether Italian or not) anywhere in Italy, and Mansell at Silverstone, but that's quasi nationalism. *Senna from Sao Paulo stirs this from Japanese women in Monte Carlo.* The global village brought him to all these different women and unites him to them, regardless of nationalities, cultures and frontiers.

For Senna this may produce a mixed reaction. As Martin Brundle says, 'it must be difficult having the constant pressure he has. He is, let's face it, one of the world's best-known people. I can trade off a relative kind of fame' — Senna can't. It's everything all at once all the time. It's the siege.

Proximity to the famous can be intoxicating and disconcerting, especially if it comes at you hard all at once and from nowhere.

Evelyn Ong from Shah Alam, Malaysia, formerly a resident of Australia:
'On that special day in November 1988 one of my brothers was leaving Melbourne for home for the summer holidays. My cousin, a friend and I were at the Tullamarine airport to see him off. I noticed a man standing near a shop window who looked familiar, as if I had seen him somewhere before. Suddenly it clicked that he looked very much like Ayrton Senna! I hesitated to approach him. He gave the impression that he wanted to be left alone.

'I called to my cousin who took one look and got very excited. My cousin said "I think it's him, what are we to do?" We had heard that Senna liked his privacy and if this man was indeed Senna he wouldn't thank us for intruding. Unexpectedly my cousin followed him into the shop. Never before have I seen my cousin deliberately approach a

169

'Somehow I feel an extraordinary presence emanates from him.' Senna between 1988 and 1994.

stranger. He asked a question. I saw the man hesitate and then answer. My cousin proceeded to shake the man's hand. When my cousin came to confirm it was Senna we were grinning a mile wide!

'We wanted a memento and, certain that Senna wouldn't want to attract attention, we sent our cousin to ask first if he minded a request for an autograph instead of charging at him. Senna agreed. We rushed into the bookshop to buy two Formula 1 magazines and Senna patiently flicked the pages till he got to a picture of himself and put his autograph there. Amazingly, nobody else noticed.'

It shows how much you can touch people.

Paulina Markovic from Berkhamsted, Hertfordshire:
'Have you really had lots of letters from women about Senna? I thought it might just be me, because most people I know think I'm crazy. I don't really know why women fall for him. For me, one reason must be his skill as a driver and he is also physically attractive, but it is his character which is so appealing. He always seems so controlled and decisive, although I get the feeling that he is probably quite an emotional person underneath. Maybe that is why women like him — because he is an enigma and we'd all like to find out what is underneath (underneath his cool exterior, not his overalls!! Or maybe that's another reason!) Plus, he has a sexy accent.'

I trust by this stage you are seeing the dimensions no man could chart and they remain valid dimensions, part of Senna and an integral part of the impact.

Renee Sharp from Newcastle upon Tyne:
'I have come under fire from many parties due to my devotion to Ayrton Senna which started in 1984 and I have to admit I was in tears on the afternoon of October 30 1988 when I saw him crossing the finishing line in first place at Suzuka to win his first World Championship. I often get the feeling that Ayrton is the recipient of hostility because he is remote and doesn't feel the need to be liked by many people, and also through downright jealousy. No other racing driver (not even Niki Lauda, who is in close running for second place) has ever stirred the almost protective feelings I have towards this remote and lonely man, even though I have been a motor racing fan from a very young age.'

There's that protective instinct again.

Carolynne Kristina of Hensall, Goole:
'I think Ayrton has changed — he seems very relaxed and much happier in himself. Last year (1992) I bombarded him with letters and he replied. I was so surprised to receive an envelope postmarked Brazil. It was a note thanking me for all the mail and for my support. This proves he cares about his fans, even British ones. I went to Silverstone this year (1993) and it was fantastic. I even made the pit-lane walkabout.

'The atmosphere was electric and I loved the noise of the cars. You can guess where I spent most of the walkabout hour, glued to the front of the McLaren garage. To see Ayrton live rather than on television driving the McLaren: what an awesome sight. He is magnificent and I loved every moment of the Grand Prix. Although I must confess I do find Ayrton very magnetic I also love Formula 1. I just find anything to do with Ayrton and Formula 1 exciting.'

'. . . a rather extraordinary presence emanates from him which even transcends the physical'

Nor can you neglect the spiritual undercurrents. *Here are three successive letters from Annie Dudley (name changed on request because 'I live my life in relative seclusion and do not seek publicity') in Adelaide, South Australia.*

8 August 1990:
'This man is unusual in so many ways, not only for his skills as a driver but in the way in which he has chosen to live his life and by his ability to adapt and change to the events which have occurred to him. My interest in motor racing is minimal but there is something special about Ayrton Senna.'

6 September 1990:
'It seems this man Senna has an unusual effect upon people — including an English writer and an obscure Australian lady — and although I have never met him, somehow I feel a rather extraordinary

'In my opinion the best part of Senna is his head and his eyes. When they appear inside his helmet there is nothing which can be compared to his stare.'

presence emanates from him which even transcends the physical. By that I mean even reading about him or seeing photographs of him, or watching him drive, if one is sensitive one is subtly aware of something different and special. I both understood and was amused by your description of mystical (author's note: in a reply letter) — amused because you seemed to be almost reluctant to admit to this, but I myself am very much aware of this quality in him.'

4 December 1993:
'Whilst I do not wish to be taken as overly pro-female, since I recognise the necessity and beauty of both men and women and what they can achieve together, I would like to make a comment on the fact that you received so many letters from women and not from men. It is my opinion that a woman would perceive Ayrton Senna in a totally different manner than a man. Men would tend to admire his driving skills, his aggression and bravery of a physical nature, and

wish to identify with him, perhaps live their lives vicariously through him; and this would appeal to the average race fan, although of course some would also admire what he stands for.

'A woman, unless she is of the nature to become infatuated with her so-called idol, tends to look behind the outer man and sees what is inside him, and what makes up the physical manifestation of his soul. She tends to be more intuitive, and desires to find in others something which goes beyond the outer cover, although I do concede that if the outer covering is attractive this man will arouse her interest initially. However, if she is of a mature outlook, this interest in his appearance will pass and she will look deeper to find out what motivates this man and why he has become what he is.

'We all need people to inspire us and we all find those who fill this role. Some of us, particularly when we are young, choose pop singers or film actors and model ourselves upon them, or we use sporting stars whose so-called heroic deeds appeal to us because they give us hope that perhaps we may be able to emulate them in some way; but as we progress we generally raise our expectations of ourselves and look for finer examples of mankind.

'We may turn to statesmen, scientists, explorers, philanthropists or religious figures. It seems we all need someone to fill that gap and drive us onwards in our evolution, and women, who are usually more aware of this journey than most men, look for these examples mostly in someone of the male gender. In Ayrton Senna they have found an ideal.

'He conducts his public life in a manner which is dignified, and his readiness to speak openly about his love for his family endears him to all women who wish men could be more open about their desires for love and tenderness. He is the complete man, who is incredibly brave, very intelligent, extremely lucid and eloquent, deeply spiritual, a loving part of a family unit and at times a playful child.

'He is also elusive to most women because they will never meet him and therefore he can never fall from grace. He will always remain something apart, something to be gazed at from afar. His image will never become tarnished in their eyes. They feel safe with him, they can keep him in their minds and never know his earthly presence where he may be able to spoil his image by becoming just an ordinary man who has habits and idiosyncrasies which at times may be annoying. He will be untainted by the familiarity of daily life.

175

Left *'Ayrton has changed. He seems very relaxed and much happier in himself.'*

Above *'Maybe that is why women like him – because he is an enigma.'*

'The lapses he has, which make him human, appeal to men who identify with this part of their own character but to women it brings out a deeper emotion. It enables them to defend him and to forgive him, both qualities of a loving mother. Maybe I am being too idealistic in my analysis of women's motives, and of course I am not so stupid as to be unaware that to many women he is their fantasy lover, but I am sure these women would not take the time to write to you but confine their thoughts to the bedroom.'

A word about the next, and final, extracts. They are selected, sensitively I hope, from many letters from Laura Giglio who lives near Milan and they go deep into the undercurrents. This is the impact on a total stranger, connected to Senna only through the umbilical cord of the global village:

'I'll miss that McLaren car with its bright colours. I liked the red and white a lot and the Williams are not so attractive. Never mind, because the other colours I've always found absolutely gorgeous are the ones on Senna's helmet. The yellow, green and blue of the Brazilian flag are splendidly shaped. I am very fond of that helmet and, of course, what it protects. That, in my opinion, is the best part of Senna, his head and his eyes. When they appear inside his helmet there is nothing which can be compared to his stare. You can feel the tension, the power that comes out of it fixed on the racecourse, and they speak for Senna's nervousness when they start blinking.

'He isn't real to me. He is kind of a dream: distant and untouchable. (Compare with the quotation at the head of the chapter, which Laura Giglio hadn't read and therefore was not mimicking.) I'll never meet him and somehow I feel I wouldn't like doing so. He is so perfect that I would be frightened to be introduced to such a man. Dreams do not do any damage however deep they may be, as long as you remember they are dreams and cannot be mixed with reality. I think that when a person stops dreaming they stop living.

'. . . *in defeat he was magnificent . . . He looked like a hurt lion and I liked him so much'*

'It isn't something "physical" that compels me to follow his career. It's in his eyes, something very deep inside which tells me he is different from other men. It's his stubbornness to give always the best of himself. When he is in the car I would like to be with him just to hold a hand on his head like a Guardian Angel to protect him.

'Physically speaking, I feel nervous and tensed until a race is over and if something happens to him it's like I'd been hurt in his place. That time when he was almost unconscious in his car after the Brazilian Grand Prix and he came out with an aching arm I felt really ill and that sensation disappeared only when I read he was getting better. I'm not only watching him. I'm there. If the Williams car proves to be so good next season (1994) there will be something I'll miss: Senna's almost unreal figure standing on the edge of the circuit watching his fellow drivers passing any time his car left him "on foot".

'Even in defeat he was magnificent. What was he feeling inside? Rage, delusion, desire to give up everything? He looked like a hurt lion and I liked him so much in those moments. I wasn't happy because he was out of the race, no. Maybe I felt more desperate than him but somehow I preferred that vision to the sight of him on the podium. On the edge of the circuit he looked so powerless and defenceless, almost like a child robbed. I wish I could have been there then.

'Every day after lunch or supper I do crosswords or read. I've noticed that on any printed paper that comes to hand there's something related to Senna to the point that in choosing what to read I deliberately try to pick material which won't have any connection with him. Even if I do that at lunchtime, later in the day something always happens which obliges me to take notice he's still there. It could be a book or something I see on TV when, if nothing else, they mention Brazil, or during a soccer game I see the advertisement 'Brasilia' peeping from among the other adverts. Even when I feel sure I'm closing the evening safely, I discover that (as recently) a soccer player is called McLaren. If I escape from books, crosswords, sports news, TV broadcasts and all other things that could remind me of him, it's my family who start talking about him.

'It happens sometimes that I have to go far from home and even those times I'm not left alone. One of these trips proved rather shocking. I accompanied an old woman to visit her husband's grave and on the way out of the cemetery she asked us to take a different path. She stopped to show me the tombstone of some distant relative of hers and next to it, in huge golden letters, I read the name SENNA. I held my breath and I felt almost ill for some seconds.

'Another time I was travelling with my daughter and we were in a hurry — we risked missing the train. I was also angry because she obliged me to stop and look at a poster display of her favourite singer. She started turning the posters and suddenly, almost at the end, the picture of Senna, dressed in his race suit, smiled at me behind the plastic cover. I uttered a cry and my daughter said "see? I've done the right thing making you stop".

'Do you remember that time Mansell 'lost' his wheel during the pit stop in Portugal? Well, before the event took place (a few seconds) I felt an inner voice telling me "something's going to happen and Mansell will be out". Again during the following Suzuka race I had that strange sensation. Mansell was behind Senna and at a certain point I felt myself thinking "if it goes on like this, next lap Mansell will be out". And it went like that. I wasn't hoping, mind you, it was something I couldn't control: it came out of my mind by itself.

'This thing of finding Senna daily in my way provoked me to try and see if it was something more than coincidence. We have a State Lottery where you bet numbers on 10 different towns and on

179

Saturdays there is a draw, five numbers from each town. I took Senna's year of birth — 1960 — and I chose one town. I promised myself that, if the number came up, I'd accept it as the answer I'd asked for. On the Saturday I almost fell out of the armchair when, on TV, among the five numbers shown of the town I'd chosen out of 90 numbers the "60" appeared, leaving me breathless and the winner of a small amount. It had never happened to me before. I do not believe in these things anyway and therefore, in spite of my promise, I told myself it had been a silly game and a meaningless coincidence . . .'

Clearly danger plays a significant part in the appeal of any driver. Many sports are dangerous, although perhaps only three — boxing, Alpine ski-racing, and motorsport — are regularly and intrinsically life-threatening. I write these words a couple of days after Ulrike Maier, 26-year-old mother, died after crashing in a downhill at Garmisch-Partenkirchen, her head striking part of the protective wall. I remember covering a downhill in 1975 and in practise for it a Frenchman called Michel Dujon struck a pylon, shattering his helmet and killing him. The same eerie whisper-rumour-silence settles over a ski resort as it does over a motor racing circuit when this happens. Since then, death has stabbed the skiers: an Italian, Leonardo David, in 1979, the Austrian Josef Walcher in 1984, the Austrian Gernot Reinstadler in 1991.

Boxing is rigorous in its application of medical fitness and referees stopping fights before serious damage is done, and in the Olympics they wear head-guards; but the deaths remain: wan, slender Johnny Owen . . .

You can contrast motor racing and from a long list select at random Gilles Villeneuve, Ronnie Peterson, Elio de Angelis, Ricardo Paletti, Manfred Winkelhock, Stefan Bellof, Paul Warwick.

But: death seemed to have stayed in abeyance in Formula 1. Paletti was the last to die in a race — Montreal 1982 — and de Angelis the last to die in a Formula 1 car testing at Paul Ricard, 1986. Scant consolation.

Safety has increased in a genuinely revolutionary sense although you may argue that good fortune has played a hand. Gerhard Berger was totally lucky when he hit the wall at Imola in 1989, his Ferrari consumed in a fireball despite superb fire marshalling and the reaction-speed of medical help. Martin Donnelly was lucky beyond

'I find the cars uncompromisingly, almost painfully, beautiful.'

credulity when his Lotus wrenched itself to pieces in Spain, Derek Warwick was extremely lucky when his Arrows flipped at Monza in 1990 grinding his helmet along the surface of the track. Riccardo Patrese was totally lucky at Estoril in 1992 when he travelled a long way airborne, passed under the pedestrian bridge and landed on the track rather than spread-eagled down the pit lane with all that that would have involved. Christian Fittipaldi was staggeringly lucky at Monza in 1993 when his Minardi looped-the-loop.

The danger is diminished, but never eradicated. The appeal of a motor race is manifold but pivots, surely, on the danger. If it wasn't dangerous it would become something else, would become Agassi taking his shirt off . . .

Estoril, that chilly day in January 1994 and along comes irreverent Johnny Herbert, largely unnoticed beyond the Senna siege. We fall to banter (the proper way to communicate with Herbert) and in the course of it I explain I'd forgotten how narrow the start-finish straight is, how pronounced the slope, how savage the turn into Turn One: and (true) confess that I hold an admiration for anyone who'll get into one of those goddamned cars and take it on.

I recount that one time at Wimbledon I interviewed a tennis player and during the course of it tried to explain that my benchmark is a Formula 1 driver. Applying that to tennis, if you get your 'backhand' wrong once you might need a wheelchair, if you're not so lucky you won't require even that. If your 'racket' breaks, through no fault of your own, you're essentially helpless and maybe into something which will break your body. Herbert, perceptive, nodded, understanding it, understanding that if the tennis player gets his backhand wrong he's love-fifteen or whatever, no further physical consequences, but if the Formula 1 driver gets Turn One wrong or the car breaks . . .

. . . the racing driver cannot escape the knowledge that dangers are always present

Motor racing has an acute edge. This part is very primitive: a man risks his life for his desires. It is the ultimate in macho — in rutting, if you like. Few women experience the need to do this: a handful of boxers, and the occasional female motor racer who doesn't tend to get very far in the big league (not enough physical strength). Perhaps only the Alpine racers run the same mortal risks as the men, and pay the same price.

Whatever his rationale, the racing driver cannot escape the knowledge that dangers are always present. He witnesses others crashing and experiences crashes himself. He sees, in the pit lane, Jacques Laffite hobbling after an accident so long ago, Clay Regazzoni in a wheelchair, Philippe Streiff paralysed — *and no safety regulations on earth can guarantee that the kevlar, the computers, the sand traps, the armco, the marshals and the medi-vac teams will protect you from the consequences.*

Herbert limps. Donnelly speaks with a hoarse voice which literally echoes his crash. Herbert and Donnelly are lucky. The true measure: Herbert still drives, Donnelly (who runs his own racing team now) lived to prove he could get back in a Formula 1 car. How do you explain this desire? I can't because I've never felt anything so strongly and the only comparison beyond ski racing and boxing which I can find is bullfighting. I'm indebted to Maurice Hamilton for suggesting the comparison and Vicky Canas of the newspaper *El Pais* for fulfilling it.

'Spaniards do not regard bullfighting as sport but a part of their cultural heritage. Between 30 and 40 per cent of the crowd are women.'

What attracts them to it?

'The emotion of the occasion, the excitement which the crowd generates and don't forget you have a band there which adds to the atmosphere. The whole atmosphere is very exciting.'

Do women feel maternal and protective towards the bullfighters?

'Yes, because of the danger.'

Does a bullfighter's 'uniform' make him more attractive?

'No doubt, no doubt of that at all. We call it a suit of lights. A bull-fighter might not look good in an ordinary suit, but in this he does and there's a ritual element to his putting it on.'

Are women turned on by bullfighters?

'Yes, completely. I asked a female friend who is a fan and, although she confirmed this, she found difficulty explaining why. Many of the bullfighters are not handsome in the way that, say, Harrison Ford is and their attraction is quite different from movie stars. What the bullfighter does — and what the racing driver does — is real. They face genuine danger, they don't have stunt men.'

Is there a particular bullfighter who is the equivalent of Senna — rich, talented and stirring deep undercurrents?

'Since the very beginning of bullfighting there have always been one or two like this. Twenty five years ago they probably couldn't read and write but now there is a school for young bullfighters in Madrid so that has improved.'

Aspects of Senna: child-prisoner of the siege, smouldering eyes and a vulnerable amiability, a logic to daunt, a fragile man of huge strength, at peace and at war with many others, as they came. And how they came: not just Prost and Irvine but Mansell and Balestre, errant back-markers in disarming quantities, and a spectacular interview with Jackie Stewart which went seismic. At the same time he is giving to the children of Brazil some of the riches he has gained; founding a business with a brand name *Driven to Perfection*; and speaking of seeing God on the last corner of Suzuka when he won the World Championship for the first time.

He guards his privacy hard, although, inevitably, he's been seen here and there with a beautiful girl on his arm since his divorce from the bride he married young, Liliane. He travels to and from circuits in helicopters and has his own jet capable of long distance flying. He enjoys the perils of jet ski-ing and evidently still flies his model aeroplanes. The rest? It's hidden behind the walls of the siege.

Some people are born to fulfil themselves in a certain medium and only need to find it. When they get there they know what to do. A ballerina, a stage, *my* stage. Agassi at Wimbledon, centre court, striptease, *my* stage. Eusebio, a leopard of a footballer down the road at Benfica in the Stadium of Light — which you pass to get to Estoril — *my* stage.

Jo Ramirez naturally confines himself to drivers. 'I do believe it is something you have from birth. I've been in motor racing for 32 years and I've been lucky to have been associated with probably five of the best drivers ever — Fangio, Clark, Stewart, Prost and Senna. I've worked with Stewart, Prost and Senna. Those three are the same as Fangio and Clark, they had it from birth, that ability to do something better than the rest. You have drivers like Mansell, Graham Hill, and James Hunt who got there by pure, sheer determination and hard work.'

Many times we've seen Mansell either collapse or be on the point of collapse after a race while Senna stands beside him on the podium impassive, composed, having driven the same distance.

'I've never seen Prost sweat in a race and Ayrton doesn't sweat much. The racing comes so naturally to them.'

Senna: He sits at the end of the table on the chilled January day in 1994, the wind sneaking and shivering through canvas sheets held by metal pegs driven into the tarmacadam of the paddock, sits easy although soon he'll be back in the Williams, risking it — the camber of the start-finish straight dipping to alter the composition of your stomach, the savage wrench into Turn One where your eyeballs wonder why they don't focus clearly any more — but on the big scale it's no more than another afternoon, another exploration, conducted to the rules every driver and no tennis player knows: *at 320kph nothing can guarantee your self-preservation.*

What to ask him before he goes? More questions? More voyeurism? How much more can he give in words? He sits, homely in the antiseptic English way, deferential, sure of himself but no flaunting, a strung-out contemplation of a creed and a life: slack but still on the Savannah, taut to any move and counter-move. He will go, any minute now, to the car, the crew and the rest of his life, holding the balance as he goes.

What more do you want of any human being?

Ayrton Senna's Full Racing Record

(P = pole position; Fl = fastest lap; R = retired; Dns = did not start; Dis = disqualified)

1973

1 Jul	First kart race	Interlagos	1

1977

S American championships	1

1978

S American championships			1
Brazilian championships			1
13-17 Sep	World Karts	Le Mans	6

1979

Brazilian championships			1
18-23 Sep	World Karts	Estoril	2

1980

Brazilian championships			1
17-21 Sep	World Karts	Nivelles, Belgium	2

1981

(P&O = P&O Ferries; T.T. = Townsend Thoresen)

Brazilian championships		Formula Ford 1600 (Van Diemen)		1
1 Mar	P&O	Brands Hatch	Van Diemen RF80-Ford	5
8 Mar	T.T.	Thruxton	Van Diemen RF81-Ford	3
15 Mar	T.T.	Brands Hatch	Van Diemen RF81-Ford	1
22 Mar	T.T.	Mallory	Van Diemen RF81-Ford	2/P
5 Apr	T.T.	Mallory	Van Diemen RF81-Ford	2
3 May	T.T.	Snetterton	Van Diemen RF81-Ford	2/P
24 May	RAC	Oulton Park	Van Diemen RF81-Ford	1/Fl
25 May	T.T.	Mallory	Van Diemen RF81-Ford	1
7 June	T.T.	Snetterton	Van Diemen RF81-Ford	1/Fl
21 June	RAC	Silverstone	Van Diemen RF81-Ford	2
27 June	T.T.	Oulton Park	Van Diemen RF81-Ford	1/Fl
4 Jul	RAC	Donington	Van Diemen RF81-Ford	1/Fl
12 Jul	RAC	Brands Hatch	Van Diemen RF81-Ford	4/Fl
25 Jul	T.T.	Oulton	Van Diemen RF81-Ford	1/Fl
26 Jul	RAC	Mallory	Van Diemen RF81-Ford	1 Fl
2 Aug	T.T.	Brands	Van Diemen RF81-Ford	1
9 Aug	RAC	Snetterton	Van Diemen RF81-Ford	1/Fl
15 Aug	T.T.	Donington	Van Diemen RF81-Ford	1
31 Aug	T.T.	Thruxton	Van Diemen RF81-Ford	1/P/Fl
16-20 Sep	World Karts	Parma		4
29 Sep	T.T.	Brands Hatch	Van Diemen RF81-Ford	2/Fl

1982 Formula Ford 2000 (Rushen Green Racing)

(P.B. = Pace British FF 2000; EFDA = European 2000)

7 Mar	P.B.	Brands Hatch	Van Diemen RF82-Ford	1/P/Fl
27 Mar	P.B.	Oulton	Van Diemen RF82-Ford	1/P/Fl
28 Mar	P.B.	Silverstone	Van Diemen RF82-Ford	1/P/Fl
4 Apr	P.B.	Donington	Van Diemen RF82-Ford	1/P/Fl
9 Apr	P.B.	Snetterton	Van Diemen RF82-Ford	1/P/Fl
12 Apr	P.B.	Silverstone	Van Diemen RF82-Ford	1/P/Fl
18 Apr	EFDA	Zolder	Van Diemen RF82-Ford	P/R
2 May	EFDA	Donington	Van Diemen RF82-Ford	1/P/Fl
3 May	P.B.	Mallory	Van Diemen RF82-Ford	1/Fl
9 May	EFDA	Zolder	Van Diemen RF82-Ford	P/F1/R
30 May	P.B.	Oulton	Van Diemen RF82-Ford	R
30 May	Celebrity	Oulton	Sunbeam Talbot T1	1/Fl

31 May	P.B.	Brands Hatch	Van Diemen RF82-Ford	1/Fl
6 June	P.B.	Mallory	Van Diemen RF82-Ford	1/Fl
13 June	P.B.	Brands Hatch	Van Diemen RF82-Ford	1/Fl
20 June	EFDA	Hockenheim	Van Diemen RF82-Ford	P/R
26 June	P.B.	Oulton	Van Diemen RF82-Ford	1/Fl
3 Jul	EFDA	Zandvoort	Van Diemen RF82-Ford	1/P
4 Jul	P.B.	Snetterton	Van Diemen RF82-Ford	2
10 Jul	P.B.	Castle Combe	Van Diemen RF82-Ford	1/P/Fl
1 Aug	P.B.	Snetterton	Van Diemen RF82-Ford	1 Fl
8 Aug	EFDA	Hockenheim	Van Diemen RF82-Ford	1/P/Fl
15 Aug	EFDA	Osterreichring	Van Diemen RF82-Ford	1/P/Fl
22 Aug	EFDA	Jyllandsring	Van Diemen RF82-Ford	1/P/Fl
30 Aug	P.B.	Thruxton	Van Diemen RF82-Ford	1/Fl
5 Sep	P.B.	Silverstone	Van Diemen RF82-Ford	1/Fl
12 Sep	EFDA	Mondello Park	Van Diemen RF82-Ford	1/Fl
15-19 Sep	World Karts	Kalmar, Sweden		14
26 Sep	P.B.	Brands Hatch	Van Diemen RF82-Ford	2/Fl
13 Nov	Formula 3	Thruxton	Ralt RT3-Toyota	1/P/Fl

1983 Marlboro British Formula 3 Championship
(West Surrey Racing except Macau when he drove for Marlboro/Teddy Yip)

6 Mar	M.B.	Silverstone	Ralt RT3-Toyota	1/Fl
13 Mar	M.B.	Thruxton	Ralt RT3-Toyota	1/P
20 Mar	M.B.	Silverstone	Ralt RT3-Toyota	1/P/Fl
27 Mar	M.B.	Donington	Ralt RT3-Toyota	1/P/Fl
4 Apr	M.B.	Thruxton	Ralt RT3-Toyota	1/P
24 Apr	M.B.	Silverstone	Ralt RT3-Toyota	1/P/Fl
2 May	M.B.	Thruxton	Ralt RT3-Toyota	1/P/Fl
8 May	M.B.	Brands Hatch	Ralt RT3-Toyota	1/P/Fl
30 May	M.B.	Silverstone	Ralt RT3-Toyota	1/P/Fl
12 June	M.B.	Silverstone	Ralt RT3-Toyota	R
19 June	M.B.	Cadwell Park	Ralt RT3-Toyota	P/Dns
3 Jul	M.B.	Snetterton	Ralt RT3-Toyota	Fl/ R
16 Jul	M.B.	Silverstone	Ralt RT3-Toyota	1/P/Fl
24 Jul	M.B.	Donington	Ralt RT3-Toyota	2/P/Fl
6 Aug	M.B.	Oulton	Ralt RT3-Toyota	Fl/R
29 Aug	M.B.	Silverstone	Ralt RT3-Toyota	1/P
11 Sep	M.B.	Oulton	Ralt RT3-Toyota	R
18 Sep	M.B.	Thruxton	Ralt RT3-Toyota	P/R

2 Oct	M.B.	Silverstone	Ralt RT3-Toyota	2
20 Oct	Macau GP	Macau	Ralt RT3-Toyota	1 P/Fl
27 Oct	M.B.	Thruxton	Ralt RT3-Toyota	1/P/Fl

1984 Formula 1

(Toleman Group Motorsport except 12 May, Nurburgring, Daimler Benz AG;
and 15 July, Nurburgring, Joest Racing Porsche 956)

25 Mar	Brazilian GP	Rio	Toleman TG183B-Hart	R
7 Apr	S. African GP	Kyalami	Toleman TG183B-Hart	6
29 Apr	Belgian GP	Zolder	Toleman TG183B-Hart	6
6 May	San Marino GP	Imola	Toleman TG183B-Hart	R
12 May	Inaugural SCR	Nurburgring	Mercedes Benz 190E	1
20 May	French GP	Dijon	Toleman TG184-Hart	R
3 June	Monaco GP	Monte Carlo	Toleman TG184-Hart	2/Fl
17 June	Canadian GP	Montreal	Toleman TG184-Hart	7
24 June	Detroit GP	Detroit	Toleman TG184-Hart	R
8 July	Dallas GP	Dallas	Toleman TG184-Hart	R
15 July	N-ring 1000 kms	Nurburgring	Porsche 956	8
22 July	British GP	Brands Hatch	Toleman TG184-Hart	3
5 Aug	German GP	Hockenheim	Toleman TG184-Hart	R
19 Aug	Austrian GP	Osterreichring	Toleman TG184-Hart	R
26 Aug	Dutch GP	Zandvoort	Toleman TG184-Hart	R
9 Sep	Italian GP	Monza	Toleman TG184-Hart	Dns
7 Oct	European GP	Nurburgring	Toleman TG184-Hart	R
21 Oct	Portuguese GP	Estoril	Toleman TG184-Hart	3

1985

7 Apr	Brazilian GP	Rio	Lotus 97T-Renault	R
21 Apr	Portuguese GP	Estoril	Lotus 97T-Renault	1/P/Fl
5 May	San Marino GP	Imola	Lotus 97T-Renault	7/P
19 May	Monaco GP	Monte Carlo	Lotus 97T-Renault	P/R
16 June	Canadian GP	Montreal	Lotus 97T-Renault	16/Fl
23 June	Detroit GP	Detroit	Lotus 97T-Renault	P/Fl/R
7 Jul	French GP	Paul Ricard	Lotus 97T-Renault	R
21 Jul	British GP	Silverstone	Lotus 97T-Renault	10
4 Aug	German GP	Nurburgring	Lotus 97T-Renault	R
18 Aug	Austrian GP	Osterreichring	Lotus 97T-Renault	2
25 Aug	Dutch GP	Zandvoort	Lotus 97T-Renault	3
8 Sep	Italian GP	Monza	Lotus 97T-Renault	3/P

15 Sep	Belgian GP	Spa	Lotus 97T-Renault	1
6 Oct	European GP	Brands Hatch	Lotus 97T-Renault	2/P
19 Oct	S. African GP	Kyalami	Lotus 97T-Renault	R
3 Nov	Australian GP	Adelaide	Lotus 97T-Renault	P/R

1986

23 Mar	Brazilian GP	Rio	Lotus 98T-Renault	2/P
13 Apr	Spanish GP	Jerez	Lotus 98T-Renault	1/P
27 Apr	San Marino GP	Imola	Lotus 98T-Renault	P/R
11 May	Monaco GP	Monte Carlo	Lotus 98T-Renault	3
25 May	Belgian GP	Spa	Lotus 98T-Renault	2
15 June	Canadian GP	Montreal	Lotus 98T-Renault	5
22 June	Detroit GP	Detroit	Lotus 98T-Renault	1/P
6 Jul	French GP	Paul Ricard	Lotus 98T-Renault	P/R
13 Jul	British GP	Brands Hatch	Lotus 98T-Renault	R
27 Jul	German GP	Hockenheim	Lotus 98T-Renault	2
10 Aug	Hungarian GP	Hungaroring	Lotus 98T-Renault	2/P
17 Aug	Austrian GP	Osterreichring	Lotus 98T-Renault	R
7 Sep	Italian GP	Monza	Lotus 98T-Renault	R
21 Sep	Portuguese GP	Estoril	Lotus 98T-Renault	4/P
12 Oct	Mexican GP	Mexico City	Lotus 98T-Renault	3/P
26 Oct	Australian GP	Adelaide	Lotus 98T-Renault	R

1987

12 Apr	Brazilian GP	Rio	Lotus 99T-Honda	R
3 May	San Marino GP	Imola	Lotus 99T-Honda	2/P
17 May	Belgian GP	Spa	Lotus 99T-Honda	R
31 May	Monaco GP	Monte Carlo	Lotus 99T-Honda	1/Fl
21 June	Detroit GP	Detroit	Lotus 99T-Honda	1/Fl
5 Jul	French GP	Paul Ricard	Lotus 99T-Honda	4
12 Jul	British GP	Silverstone	Lotus 99T-Honda	3
26 Jul	German GP	Hockenheim	Lotus 99T-Honda	3
9 Aug	Hungarian GP	Hungaroring	Lotus 99T-Honda	2
16 Aug	Austrian GP	Osterreichring	Lotus 99T-Honda	5
6 Sep	Italian GP	Monza	Lotus 99T-Honda	2/Fl
20 Sep	Portuguese GP	Estoril	Lotus 99T-Honda	7
27 Sep	Spanish GP	Jerez	Lotus 99T-Honda	5
18 Oct	Mexican GP	Mexico City	Lotus 99T-Honda	R
1 Nov	Japanese GP	Suzuka	Lotus 99T-Honda	2

15 Nov	Australian GP	Adelaide	Lotus 99T-Honda	R

1988 – *World Champion*

3 Apr	Brazilian GP	Rio	McLaren MP4/4 Honda	P/Dis
1 May	San Marino GP	Imola	McLaren MP4/4 Honda	1/P
15 May	Monaco GP	Monte Carlo	McLaren MP4/4 Honda	P/Fl/R
29 May	Mexican GP	Mexico City	McLaren MP4/4 Honda	2/P
12 June	Canadian GP	Montreal	McLaren MP4/4 Honda	1/P/Fl
19 June	Detroit GP	Detroit	McLaren MP4/4 Honda	1/P
3 Jul	French GP	Paul Ricard	McLaren MP4/4 Honda	2
10 Jul	British GP	Silverstone	McLaren MP4/4 Honda	1
24 Jul	German GP	Hockenheim	McLaren MP4/4 Honda	1/P
8 Aug	Hungarian GP	Hungaroring	McLaren MP4/4 Honda	1/P
28 Aug	Belgian GP	Spa	McLaren MP4/4 Honda	1/P
11 Sep	Italian GP	Monza	McLaren MP4/4 Honda	P/R
25 Sep	Portuguese GP	Estoril	McLaren MP4/4 Honda	6
2 Oct	Spanish GP	Jerez	McLaren MP4/4 Honda	4/P
30 Oct	Japanese GP	Suzuka	McLaren MP4/4 Honda	1/P/Fl
13 Nov	Australian GP	Adelaide	McLaren MP4/4 Honda	2/P

1989

26 Mar	Brazilian GP	Rio	McLaren MP4/5 Honda	11/P
23 Apr	San Marino GP	Imola	McLaren MP4/5 Honda	1/P
7 May	Monaco GP	Monte Carlo	McLaren MP4/5 Honda	1/P
28 May	Mexican GP	Mexico City	McLaren MP4/5 Honda	1/P
4 June	American GP	Phoenix	McLaren MP4/5 Honda	P/Fl/R
18 June	Canadian GP	Montreal	McLaren MP4/5 Honda	R
9 Jul	French GP	Paul Ricard	McLaren MP4/5 Honda	R
16 Jul	British GP	Silverstone	McLaren MP4/5 Honda	P/R
30 Jul	German GP	Hockenheim	McLaren MP4/5 Honda	1/P/Fl
13 Aug	Hungarian GP	Hungaroring	McLaren MP4/5 Honda	2
27 Aug	Belgian GP	Spa	McLaren MP4/5 Honda	1/P
10 Sept	Italian GP	Monza	McLaren MP4/5 Honda	P/R
24 Sept	Portuguese GP	Estoril	McLaren MP4/5 Honda	P/R
1 Oct	Spanish GP	Jerez	McLaren MP4/5 Honda	1/P/Fl
22 Oct	Japanese GP	Suzuka	McLaren MP4/5 Honda	P/Fl/Dis
5 Nov	Australian GP	Adelaide	McLaren MP4/5 Honda	P/R

1990 – *World Champion*

11 Mar	American GP	Phoenix	McLaren MP4/5B Honda	1

25 Mar	Brazilian GP	Interlagos	McLaren MP4/5B Honda	3/P
13 May	San Marino GP	Imola	McLaren MP4/5B Honda	P/R
27 May	Monaco GP	Monte Carlo	McLaren MP4/5B Honda	1/P/Fl
10 June	Canadian GP	Montreal	McLaren MP4/5B Honda	1/P
24 June	Mexican GP	Mexico City	McLaren MP4/5B Honda	R
8 Jul	French GP	Paul Ricard	McLaren MP4/5B Honda	3
15 Jul	British GP	Silverstone	McLaren MP4/5B Honda	3
29 Jul	German GP	Hockenheim	McLaren MP4/5B Honda	1/P
12 Aug	Hungarian GP	Hungaroring	McLaren MP4/5B Honda	2
26 Aug	Belgian GP	Spa	McLaren MP4/5B Honda	1/P
9 Sept	Italian GP	Monza	McLaren MP4/5B Honda	1/P/Fl
23 Sept	Portuguese GP	Estoril	McLaren MP4/5B Honda	2
30 Sept	Spanish GP	Jerez	McLaren MP4/5B Honda	P/R
21 Oct	Japanese GP	Suzuka	McLaren MP4/5B Honda	P/R
4 Nov	Australian GP	Adelaide	McLaren MP4/5B Honda	P/R

1991 – *World Champion*

10 Mar	American GP	Phoenix	McLaren MP4/6 Honda	1/P
24 Mar	Brazilian GP	Interlagos	McLaren MP4/6 Honda	1/P
28 Apr	San Marino GP	Imola	McLaren MP4/6 Honda	1/P
12 May	Monaco GP	Monte Carlo	McLaren MP4/6 Honda	1/P
2 June	Canadian GP	Montreal	McLaren MP4/6 Honda	R
16 June	Mexican GP	Mexico City	McLaren MP4/6 Honda	3
7 Jul	French GP	Magny Cours	McLaren MP4/6 Honda	3
14 Jul	British GP	Silverstone	McLaren MP4/6 Honda	4
28 Jul	German GP	Hockenheim	McLaren MP4/6 Honda	7
11 Aug	Hungarian GP	Hungaroring	McLaren MP4/6 Honda	1/P
25 Aug	Belgian GP	Spa	McLaren MP4/6 Honda	1/P
8 Sep	Italian GP	Monza	McLaren MP4/6 Honda	2/P/Fl
22 Sep	Portuguese GP	Estoril	McLaren MP4/6 Honda	2
29 Sep	Spanish GP	Jerez	McLaren MP4/6 Honda	5
20 Oct	Japanese GP	Suzuka	McLaren MP4/6 Honda	2/Fl
3 Nov	Australian GP	Adelaide	McLaren MP4/6 Honda	1/P

1992

1 Mar	S African GP	Kyalami	McLaren MP4/6B Honda	3
22 Mar	Mexican GP	Mexico City	McLaren MP4/6B Honda	R
5 Apr	Brazilian GP	Interlagos	McLaren MP4/7A Honda	R
3 May	Spanish GP	Barcelona	McLaren MP4/7A Honda	9

17 May	San Marino GP	Imola	McLaren MP4/7A Honda	3
31 May	Monaco GP	Monte Carlo	McLaren MP4/7A Honda	1
14 June	Canadian GP	Montreal	McLaren MP4/7A Honda	R/P
5 Jul	French GP	Magny Cours	McLaren MP4/7A Honda	R
12 Jul	British GP	Silverstone	McLaren MP4/7A Honda	R
26 Jul	German GP	Hockenheim	McLaren MP4/7A Honda	2
16 Aug	Hungarian GP	Hungaroring	McLaren MP4/7A Honda	1
30 Aug	Belgian GP	Spa	McLaren MP4/7A Honda	5
13 Sept	Italian GP	Monza	McLaren MP4/7A Honda	1
27 Sept	Portuguese GP	Estoril	McLaren MP4/7A Honda	3/Fl
25 Oct	Japanese GP	Suzuka	McLaren MP4/7A Honda	R
8 Nov	Australian GP	Adelaide	McLaren MP4/7A Honda	R

1993

14 Mar	S. African GP	Kyalami	McLaren MP4/8 Ford	2
28 Mar	Brazilian GP	Interlagos	McLaren MP4/8 Ford	1
11 Apr	European GP	Donington	McLaren MP4/8 Ford	1/Fl
25 Apr	San Marino GP	Imola	McLaren MP4/8 Ford	R
9 May	Spanish GP	Barcelona	McLaren MP4/8 Ford	2
23 May	Monaco GP	Monte Carlo	McLaren MP4/8 Ford	1
13 June	Canadian GP	Montreal	McLaren MP4/8 Ford	R
4 Jul	French GP	Magny Cours	McLaren MP4/8 Ford	4
11 Jul	British GP	Silverstone	McLaren MP4/8 Ford	5
25 Jul	German GP	Hockenheim	McLaren MP4/8 Ford	4
15 Aug	Hungarian GP	Hungaroring	McLaren MP4/8 Ford	R
29 Aug	Belgian GP	Spa	McLaren MP4/8 Ford	4
12 Sep	Italian GP	Monza	McLaren MP4/8 Ford	R
26 Sep	Portuguese GP	Estoril	McLaren MP4/8 Ford	R
24 Oct	Japanese GP	Suzuka	McLaren MP4/8 Ford	1
7 Nov	Australian GP	Adelaide	McLaren MP4/8 Ford	1/P

1994

27 Mar	Brazilian GP	Interlagos	Williams FW16 Renault	P/R
17 Apr	Pacific GP	Aida	Williams FW16 Renault	P/R
1 May	San Marino GP	Imola	Williams FW16 Renault	P/killed